I'm Fine!

Text copyright © Wendy Billington 2013
The author asserts the moral right to be identified as the author of this work

Published by
The Bible Reading Fellowship
15 The Chambers, Vineyard
Abingdon OX14 3FE
United Kingdom
Tel: +44 (0)1865 319700
Email: enquiries@brf.org.uk
Website: www.brf.org.uk
BRF is a Registered Charity

ISBN 978 1 84101 871 3

First published 2013

10 9 8 7 6 5 4 3 2 1 0

Acknowledgments
Unless otherwise stated, scripture quotations are taken from The Holy Bible, New International Version (Anglicised edition), copyright © 1979, 1984, 2011 by Biblica (formerly International Bible Society), and are used by permission of Hodder & Stoughton Publishers, an Hachette UK company. All rights reserved. 'NIV' is a registered trademark of Biblica (formerly International Bible Society). UK trademark number 1448790.

A catalogue record for this book is available from the British Library

Printed and bound by CPI Group (UK) Ltd, Croydon CR0 4YY

I'm
fine!

Removing masks and growing
into wholeness

Wendy Billington

Acknowledgments

I would like to express my appreciation to the individuals who have so willingly contributed their own personal stories to this book. My writings are based around these stories and they have helped bring a rich dimension to the issues addressed. In the interest of confidentiality, names have been changed and these people cannot be identified.

The book is dedicated to these contributors and to my dear friends within my church and the Sevenoaks Christian Counselling Service, whose friendship and support I have much valued.

I am especially indebted to my friend Jean Watson for the practical help and encouragement she has given me, without which the book would have been the poorer.

Contents

From Psalm 139 (of David), for reflection

You have searched me, Lord,
and you know me.
You know when I sit and when I rise;
you perceive my thoughts from afar.
You discern my going out and my lying down;
you are familiar with all my ways.
Before a word is on my tongue
you, Lord, know it completely.
You hem me in behind and before,
and you lay your hand upon me.
Such knowledge is too wonderful for me,
too lofty for me to attain.

Where can I go from your Spirit?
Where can I flee from your presence?
If I go up to the heavens, you are there;
if I make my bed in the depths, you are there.
If I rise on the wings of the dawn,
if I settle on the far side of the sea,
even there your hand will guide me,
your right hand will hold me fast...

For you created my inmost being;
you knit me together in my mother's womb.
I praise you because I am fearfully and wonderfully made;
your works are wonderful,
I know that full well.

My frame was not hidden from you
when I was made in the secret place,
when I was woven together in the depths of the earth.
Your eyes saw my unformed body;
all the days ordained for me were written in your book
before one of them came to be…

Search me, God, and know my heart;
test me and know my anxious thoughts.
See if there is any offensive way in me,
and lead me in the way everlasting.

Foreword

I've lost count of the number of conversations I've had in which we've agreed, 'Why aren't we more real with each other in church? Why do we hide our true feelings behind that cheesy Christian grin we think we've got to show to the world?' It's true: I realised with some horror, a few years ago, that I had experienced a greater depth of honesty and warmth of compassion and acceptance within the non-Christian counselling training group to which I belonged than I had ever experienced within my church fellowship.

Yet it doesn't have to be so. In *I'm Fine!* Wendy Billington gently peels back the mask and sensitively uncovers the varied pains that might lie behind that cheesy grin and cheery 'I'm fine, thanks!'— and particularly the shame that keeps things locked away in secret. She brings lots of expertise to bear here, particularly her experience and counselling skills in pastoral care and the down-to-earth understanding and practical realism with which she writes. The many stories with which she illustrates the issues are deeply moving. I challenge you not to be moved to tears, as I was, by Caroline's story in Chapter 6. But the best thing about Wendy's book, to my mind, is her hopefulness about the church. She really believes that churches can become places of welcome, empathy, acceptance and support where we can all dare to be real about what lies behind the mask and find the emotional and practical help we need.

Wendy recognises that this may mean calling on wider resources, and provides relevant suggestions. But behind it all, for her, lies a vision of the church of Jesus Christ truly animated by the gospel of God's grace—the good news of a waiting Father who longs to greet his shame-filled children with a loving embrace and not an accusing finger. That's encouraging!

Steve Motyer, London School of Theology

Introduction

I often wonder what is going on in the minds of people who, when asked how they are, respond by saying that they are fine. For some this *will* be the case but for others it may be far from the truth. In saying 'I'm fine!' it may be that they are unprepared or unwilling to talk—this may be inappropriate at the time for a variety of reasons—or they may need to be private about some matter; this is all quite understandable. But when they are covering up what needs attention like a wound or an infection, something that will get worse if left to fester, things are certainly not fine. Are we as individuals and churches aware of such people and ready to offer support and help? Being told to 'read the Bible and all will be well' is certainly not the whole solution.

This book considers a number of issues that affect many church members but which, for various reasons, are often hidden beneath an 'I'm fine' response. Each chapter addresses one specific issue and explores it through individual stories and experiences, suggesting what the causes might be, as well as the effects, and giving possible insights into and understanding of what might be going on. In order to encourage release for those concerned, avenues of help are suggested for the individuals themselves, through the church, and through the Bible and God himself, 'a source of strength to those who turn back the battle at the gate' (Isaiah 28:6), so that we can be drawn into a deeper relationship with him and claim the blessings he has in store for us.

This is not meant to be a 'them and us' book. It is not as though 'we' are strong and 'they' are weak, so we must help 'them'. No— we are living in an imperfect world as imperfect people. At some time in life we will all hit difficulties—through our circumstances, genes, choices or whatever—and will need help. Similarly, at some time in life, and often because we have learned through our own difficulties, we will be able to reach out and help others going through tough times. There is no need to hide behind masks of any sort, pretending to be fine. Instead we can be honest and open with one another and accept the help we need from or offer the help we can give to one another. And as Christians we have all God's resources to draw on, knowing that he cares for us and wants us to grow in freedom and wholeness.

The book is intended for anyone to read: individuals, befrienders, church ministers, pastoral carers, home group leaders and their members. There may also be those who, while not necessarily professing a Christian faith, may gain something through its chapters.

Some of the stories are of real people and are used with permission but with names and details altered in order to protect privacy; others are realistic true-to-life scenarios based on my pastoral experiences, observations and research but unrelated to any particular individual. Some of the prayers at the ends of the chapters have been written by those whose stories and experiences we have read.

For most of us it is hard to watch others struggling and trapped in lives of misery and pain. As the chapters unfold, we will see the ways in which God can use each one of us to relieve suffering and bring about change and growth.

Chapter 1

Low self-esteem: finding a sense of worth

'Are not five sparrows sold for two pennies? Yet not one of them is forgotten by God. Indeed, the very hairs of your head are all numbered. Don't be afraid; you are worth more than many sparrows.'
LUKE 12:6–7

With a healthy positive self-esteem, we are likely to be able to face the world with confidence and to be at ease and at peace with ourselves and others.

What actually is self-esteem? The dictionary gives as the definition of 'esteem' the words 'respect' and 'value'. So adding these words to 'self-' we can simply define self-esteem as an evaluation of ourselves as worthy of respect, acceptance and value. With a healthy positive self-esteem, we are likely to be able to face the world with confidence and to be at ease and at peace with ourselves, not being concerned about what others think of us. There is thus no need to hide from ourselves, from others or, as redeemed people, from God. Freed to love and serve God, we can quite genuinely say 'I'm fine!' and mean it.

Low self-esteem involves negative opinions and unpleasant feelings about ourselves which we often conceal from others. We may long to change but it is often difficult to know whether this is possible and, if it is, how to go about it. If that is our situation, life can just carry on in this unhappy state.

High self-esteem may involve inflated opinions of self-worth and value; here, treating others disparagingly may be a pattern of behaviour. This can become apparent with those who have risen high within their profession: their status has 'gone to their head'. Paradoxically those who come across as having high opinions of themselves may in fact be suffering from feelings of insecurity and hiding who they are behind a front of confidence.

It is low self-esteem we will be considering in this chapter: its causes and effects, and ways in which we can be helped towards a healthier self-esteem. As we lift our masks, change can take place and negative opinions about ourselves can be removed.

Our family background and our upbringing can be an overriding influence in determining how we value ourselves as individuals, as illustrated in George's life.

George's story (part 1)

George was brought up as a Christian but with very poor role models provided by his dysfunctional family. They all went to church together each Sunday but the people they knew were totally unaware of what went on behind their closed doors and the unhappiness in that home. It wasn't until George was about nine that he began to realise that other families functioned differently. His friends' mums and dads talked to each other in a much calmer manner and were not continually scoring points against each other. In their homes, instead of tension there was a loving and caring atmosphere. As George became more aware of the confrontations between his parents, he began to be fearful and found himself instinctively taking on the role of a go-between and communicator. On the rare occasions when he was invited into others' homes, he always enjoyed the peaceful environment they provided; gradually he became ashamed of his own home, and feelings of inferiority started to take root. He disliked his secondary school; he was unable to make friends and rarely achieved his true potential academically. Sitting tests and exams became a nightmare to him; although he knew he had the ability to do well and, in fact, better than most of his peers, his mind would freeze when he opened the exam papers.

His father had encouraged him to join the scout group attached to their church. For a while George enjoyed this immensely. He went on expeditions, gained activity awards and felt accepted and affirmed by his fellow scouts and the leaders. When he was 14, however, his mother was told by his teachers at school that George was not doing well enough, so she made him leave the scouts and concentrate on his studies. George was devastated, for he loved being a scout and this was the one area in his life where he felt 'good'—accepted and valued.

He began to look sad all the time. Once, when asked at school whether anything was bothering him he quietly replied that he was fine, knowing full well that was far from the case.

He managed to scrape a place at a minor university, thanks to the fact that entry was based on interview and general assessment and not on examination grades, but his first year there was a disaster. He felt rejected by his fellow students and especially by his tutor, who seemed to sap most of the remaining confidence from him, belittling him for his poor performance and also his Christian faith. Although outwardly George appeared to be and still said he was 'fine', inwardly he felt worthless and fearful of failing to such an extent that shortly before the end of his first year he was on the brink of leaving. His bags were packed and a letter was written and ready for posting to the principal, but just as he was discreetly leaving through the back entrance of the college, he stopped in his tracks. Would the fact that he was giving in haunt him for the rest of his life and ruin any prospect of a meaningful career or, worst of all, the prospect of marriage and a happy family? The last of these was the strongest pull, for he had always longed to be in a loving relationship, to have children and to establish the kind of secure and loving home of which he had been deprived. He walked slowly back towards his room and came to the door of the college chapel, a place he had passed umpteen times before and never entered. Little did he know his decision to open that door was to be the turning point of his life.

Causes of low self-esteem

Upbringing

Self-esteem is often rooted in upbringing and childhood experiences. Children's feelings of self-worth can be damaged when they are persistently criticised, undermined, deprived of love and physical affection and given unrealistic goals to achieve. It was not surprising that George, brought up in a dysfunctional and unhappy environment of which he was ashamed, lacked confidence and thus the ability to achieve.

The position of a sibling within a family can have a bearing on their sense of identity. The account of David's anointing as future king of Israel by Samuel is a good example of this. When Samuel visited David's father, Jesse, his father dismissed the idea that David, his youngest son, was of any importance or significance; he just tended the sheep. The other sons looked impressive but none of them was God's choice. Another example of this is the story of Joseph, Jacob's son, whose brothers were jealous because Jacob 'loved Joseph more than any of his other sons, because he had been born to him in his old age' (Genesis 37:3a), and therefore treated him with contempt. Even today, the eldest in a family might feel a sense of importance and superiority; the youngest can sometimes feel looked down on as the baby and thus develop feelings of inferiority. Children who are loved unconditionally and equally, and accepted for who they are, are more likely to develop a healthy self-esteem and be able to take their place in society with confidence. Those who have not had the privilege of this kind of upbringing, and consequently suffer from feelings of inferiority, must be helped to understand the biblical teaching on human worth (explored later in this chapter) and encouraged not to respond negatively to those wanting to affirm them.

Introvert personality

Growing up as an introvert in a church culture with an extravert bias can bring about feelings of inadequacy and low self-worth.

Our innate desire is to be accepted by others, but the experience of introverts is that they are often misunderstood, especially in their social interactions, and hence misconstrued as misfits. They process their thinking internally and consequently tend to be slower to respond, needing to withdraw from others in order to be re-energised. Thus they can come across as aloof and anti-social. Extraverts are more easily accepted by others; their gregariousness is appealing and something to be treasured. Having the same inherent desire to be loved and accepted as everyone else, those who have an introvert personality can suffer pain as they find themselves under-valued and even ignored by others. To escape the hurt of rejection, they may retreat behind their mask into their own private world.

Distorted Christian beliefs

Christian beliefs focusing heavily on our sinfulness and guilt can create feelings of worthlessness. How can we possibly value ourselves when we fall into sin daily? Added to this, Christians may feel—rightly or wrongly—that the kind of self-esteem advocated in secular society is in reality a form of pride which is at variance with the gospel message of human sinfulness and the need for humility. Such thinking can cause Christians to undervalue themselves to the detriment of their mental and emotional well-being.

Peer relationships

As an educationalist I know that the foundations of affirmation and self-worth are now included in the classroom experience; children are not normally 'put down' in the way they used to be. What happens in the playground may be another matter. Many children have unpleasant and damaging experiences of bullying, teasing and exclusion from friendship groups. As a result they can feel lonely and isolated, often hiding their pain as they spiral into feelings of low self-worth, which, if not addressed, can become embedded in them for a lifetime.

Social influences

Present-day culture places a high value on intelligence, money, physical attractiveness and success, all of which are inconsistent with biblical principles if pursued as goals in themselves. As people strive to measure up to these yardsticks and, in many cases, fail, they can start to believe that what they offer is valueless. From there it is just a short step to feeling second-rate and worthless.

Constant criticism

Constant criticism can destroy a person's self-image. Marriage is often a breeding ground for criticism when one or other partner or both are always on the attack, criticising the other person for what they do or don't do.

External events

External events often outside our control, such as losing a job, failing an interview or having poor health, can all contribute to low self-esteem.

Effects of low self-esteem

Most people at some time in their lives experience feelings of low self-esteem, but when these feelings are intense and constant, they can affect the quality not only of their own lives but also those of others.

This is how some people with low self-esteem express their thoughts and feelings:

- Most people in the church have got their act together. I haven't!
- I feel useless compared with others I know.
- I find it more difficult than others I know to form and maintain meaningful relationships.
- My parents were always putting me down and saying that I was no good. It probably still is the case.

- I dislike my looks and body. I know I should lose weight and buy some decent clothes, but I can't be bothered.
- I can't accept compliments, for I don't see them as based on fact.
- I am jealous of what others achieve.
- I want to impress others, so I often say false things about my achievements.
- I feel lonely, isolated and unloved. No one seems to want to talk to me.
- Life is such a struggle. I try hard but achieve so little.
- I don't want to share my feelings with others.
- It does help to share my pain with God, for I know he understands, values me and is with me in the pain. However, he doesn't take it away, so this is the cross I have to bear.

Some people reading this chapter may well identify with a number of these sentiments but be reluctant to come out into the open for fear of being considered weak. 'To be released from these feelings and negative thinking would be great, but I can't change now. I have been like this since I was a child. I will just accept these feelings and live with them' may well be what they say or think.

How the church can help

Love and affirm one another
Offering words of affirmation, compliments and encouragement that are genuine and honest assists people in valuing themselves. It's all about loving them with a love that is not just a vague emotion but a commitment to their well-being. The recipient may at first have difficulty in believing the truth of what is being said, but given time their mindset can change.

Encourage small networks of care
Establishing a platform of trust, acceptance and understanding can create a safe place in which to share. Prayer triplets have been an enormous encouragement to many people in my own church,

enabling bridges of friendship to be built, where masks are lifted and feelings and thoughts are shared. To be listened to, feel loved and be prayed for by caring and empathetic friends can be very powerful and a gateway to change.

Small groups can also play a useful part in helping those with low self-esteem. Most churches now have a structure of small groups in which caring relationships are established and the Bible is studied and applied to everyday life. In this way people can develop friendships and grow in confidence.

Train people in listening and pastoral skills
When self-worth has been damaged, for instance by a childhood experience, this needs to be recognised and worked through; to be able to do this with a wise and caring friend can be very beneficial. Churches can identify and help train people to befriend and get alongside others who are lonely and lack self-confidence. To be accepted and offered care and friendship in a variety of ways by a loving church family can play a major role in helping those with feelings of inferiority to move forward. As they gain in confidence, they will be motivated to start exploring ways in which they can help themselves and others too.

Teach people our value in God's eyes
So many of us are imprisoned within a mindset of worrying about what others may be thinking about us. To offer clear and applied Bible teaching to help people change from a self-focused life to a God-focused one could be the means of liberation for them, as they learn to be concerned only with how they are seen and valued by God.

How people can help themselves

As we have seen, what matters is how God values us and not the way we perceive the world valuing us. For example, these days the world values more those who are in paid employment and undervalues others who, for whatever reason, are not—mums, for instance, who stay at home to look after the family. Such values are all wrapped up in the need to succeed and achieve.

Healing the past

No one has perfect parents, but whatever the pain they have caused, however hard its effects, the damage must be worked through so that healing and wholeness can take place. We may find it difficult to forgive our parents—and we may need help with this—but when we are able to choose to open up about the past, forgive and let go of negative feelings, we will be freed to grow in confidence and wholeness.

Negative thinking

It is helpful to take note of our negative thought patterns, which affect feelings and emotions, and especially those that recur on a regular basis. Although these may be based on false assumptions, they can become entrenched within us over long periods of time. Devaluing ourselves in our minds, for example, is not right and is actually dishonouring to God. This negative thinking needs to change into positive action whereby we look to identify the gifts we have been given and use them for God's purposes. To be constantly envying others' gifts and making comparisons with our own is not what God desires of us and devalues what gifts we do have.

To keep a 'thought diary' detailing situations that may have triggered the negative thinking can be helpful. It can then be used, with a trusted friend and/or with a professional, to pinpoint and work through what has emerged.

The way we look

I find it somewhat alarming to hear a Christian say they don't care about what they look like and that people must accept them as they are. I recall my own mother bemoaning the need to buy an outfit for a special occasion, saying she wished she could wear a sack! We read of Samuel saying at the time of David's anointing,

'Man looks at the outward appearance, but the Lord looks at the heart' (1 Samuel 16:7b). However, the fact that God looks primarily at the heart doesn't mean that the body is not worth caring about. Neglect of our bodies, even in later years, has a negative effect on our self-esteem. To care for our appearance by being well groomed and well dressed gives a pleasing impression to others and says much about who we are as God's creation. Eunice found a practical means to help re-focus her thinking.

Eunice's story

I have struggled throughout my life with a poor body image. The message that God loves me just as I am was a wonderful revelation but one which has taken many years to sink in. As a result, insecurity about my appearance has too often dominated my thinking. I therefore found it very helpful to attend a beauty and style advice session where I received advice about my 'best' colours and was shown some quick make-up techniques. I now feel much more confident when I buy clothes and apply make-up and therefore waste less time and money. Best of all, though, I have subsequently received many compliments about my appearance, which have boosted my self-esteem and helped me to focus less on myself and more on the task at hand!

Regular exercise, sufficient sleep and a well-balanced diet are all-important in enabling us to function effectively in everyday life and can be seen as indicators of how we value ourselves as well as how we feel about our place both within our own human family and in God's family. Paul says, 'Do you not know that your body is a temple of the Holy Spirit, who is in you, whom you have received from God? You are not your own; you were bought at a price. Therefore honour God with your body' (1 Corinthians 6:19–20).

Relationships

Let's imagine a person who suffers from low self-worth but becomes resigned to it, saying, 'I've always been like this.' He keeps himself to himself, insisting, like George, that he's 'fine'.

I would like to make two suggestions to such a person. First, as Christians we are designed for relationships—to be loved and to love is part of being human—and therefore we need to put aside any false sense of self-sufficiency and learn to accept both love and practical help from others. Secondly I know from my own experience that when I am on the receiving end of love I become a more loving person myself. Friends bring depth and meaning to life. When a relationship between two people is unbalanced, with one giving more to it than the other, it is wise to acknowledge and address this together so that each is focused on meeting the needs of the other.

Making comparisons

Those who feel useless as they compare themselves with others would do well to reflect on the personal value and significance that they have in God's eyes and be reminded again of the truth that they are created in God's image, loved and redeemed by him and gifted in individual ways for his purposes. God does not want us to envy others' gifts but rather to identify and concentrate on the ones with which he has blessed us. Finding our rightful place in the body of Christ creates a sense of value and usefulness. We can then thank God for the gifts he has given us, asking him to show us ways in which we can use them within our church and beyond. Discovering our own personal talent may come about through chatting with someone we know well. Working through one of the exercises at the end of this chapter may be a helpful way of tackling this.

Paul says in his first letter to the Corinthians:

If the whole body were an eye, where would the sense of hearing be? If the whole body were an ear, where would the sense of smell be? But in fact God has arranged the parts in the body, every one of them, just as he wanted them to be… Now you are the body of Christ, and each one of you is a part of it. (1 Corinthians 12:17–18, 27)

Whatever our gifts, they are given to us to be used for building up the body of Christ. Jesus tells us in the parable of the talents (Matthew 25:14–30) that the talents entrusted to the master's servants varied in number but all were given to be faithfully and joyfully used.

Some people, instead of valuing the gifts they have been given, covet those of others.

John's story

John is a financial consultant and lives with his wife and two teenage children in a village in Surrey, commuting the thirty miles or so daily to central London. His father died when he was ten and he and his sister were brought up by their mother in Doncaster, her home town. Life was a struggle for her—money was always short—but she did her best to provide for herself and the children, working as a cook in the local secondary school. They were members of a local church and John became active in the youth club. He was proud to have a GP's son, Jim, as his best friend, but they lost contact when Jim followed in his father's steps and went to medical school in Nottingham. From an early age John had a chip on his shoulder, always feeling inferior to others; he was ashamed of the terrace house on a local estate where they lived and was reluctant to tell others that his mother was a school cook. Now that he had worked his way up from being a clerk in a local bank to being a financial adviser, he felt proud. However his feelings of inferiority persisted, not least because he had not been to university like most of his friends and colleagues, a fact that he was always reluctant to admit. So, in his desire to impress and achieve, he was economical with the truth and even told lies by fabricating his education and professional achievements. He was acutely aware of what he was doing, but sadly the whole situation spiralled out of control. He stopped going to church and serious tensions developed in his marriage.

In today's world, our desire to achieve can dominate our lives, with a tendency to shape our image around what we have or haven't managed to do. People who are prone to compare themselves with others are commonly heard to use phrases such as 'I'm useless', 'I'm no good', 'I'm a failure'. British culture tends to make us reluctant to blow our own trumpets and thus we have difficulty in accepting compliments. However, some, like John, try to impress others by telling half-truths or untruths about themselves. Most of us have been geared to crave success for ourselves and others. Indeed for some it's almost like a drug. And because we revere those who have been successful, what we fear most for ourselves and those we love is failure.

We are taught by Jesus that loving God and being obedient to him should take precedence over worldly success. Jesus says, 'What good will it be for a man if he gains the whole world, yet forfeits his soul?' (Matthew 16:26). If, for instance, a job application is unsuccessful or, despite our conscientiousness, we fail an exam or, as in John's case, we have no university background, we must not consider ourselves inadequate or failures. Rather, our circumstances can become fertile soil for planting the seed of hope, which can take root and produce a fruit of greater worth and significance in God's sight—something not so easily accomplished in the arid desert of overblown success.

Reacting to criticism

How we react to criticism is important, especially being able to take on board 'good' criticism. When this comes from a well-meaning friend, it is important not to be defensive but rather to accept it in the spirit in which it is meant. I personally value someone whom I know well gently telling me about a particular weakness that I show and, if appropriate, helping me towards change. A strong marriage relationship can be a good context for such learning.

A relationship with God

Healthy self-esteem can grow through the knowledge of God's unconditional love for us and our own love and dependence on him and our willingness to allow God to speak to us and live in us. Relationships—including our relationship with God—are all about spending time together and getting to know each other.

I have had periods in my life when I have felt spiritually dry, unable to talk to God, unable to *feel* he is there while knowing that he is. It is a bit like being told, 'There was a beautiful sunrise this morning', when we haven't seen it for ourselves. We can become so blinded by our problems that we are hardly aware of God's existence or the joys he has to offer. It is when we look back on episodes in our lives that we realise how God's hand has been on us through it all, guiding us in ways of which at the time we were oblivious.

How can we recapture the joy that we may feel we have lost in our relationship with God? I personally love the psalms and find it easy to identify with the psalmists; their writings express the whole range of human feelings and experience, and I often make the words and sentiments my own prayer. I find it helpful to meditate on just one thought or verse and make it my own for the day, recalling the words from time to time. I hand over to God any lurking concerns and troubles, asking him to show me how I can draw on his resources. Jesus' words about the vine and the branches are a treasure trove. He wants us to blossom and flourish; in the same way that a branch draws its vital juices from the vine, so we can draw spiritual strength through living in a close relationship with our creator. In John 15:4, Jesus says, 'Remain in me, and I will remain in you. No branch can bear fruit by itself; it must remain in the vine. Neither can you bear fruit unless you remain in me.' We have been chosen by God and called into a relationship with him where we can be loved and cherished and fed and resourced by him.

How God and the Bible can help

The Bible shows in many ways how precious we are to God and how he loves and forgives us. However, there are people I know who suffer from feelings of low self-worth and inferiority aggravated by an acute awareness of personal sin, alienation and judgment by God—a concept with which sincere Christians often struggle. How can God value us when we are displeasing him on a daily basis in our thoughts and actions? It is totally right that we should be aware of our sins and failures and confess these, but in his infinite love 'Christ Jesus came into the world to save sinners' (1 Timothy 1:15). As believers, we must recognise ourselves as *forgiven* sinners, through the cross, released from our guilt and loved and valued by our heavenly Father, from whom we are no longer separated. With this changed status as members of God's family, we can set aside feelings of worthlessness and value ourselves as redeemed people uniquely created for his purposes.

God-given responsibilities

God trusts us with responsibilities, and this helps us to value ourselves. Our value to God is affirmed in many ways within the Bible; for instance, in the responsibilities he has given us to care for his creation. There are references throughout the Bible that remind us how important we are to God: 'You made them [human beings] a little lower than the angels; you crowned them with glory and honour and put everything under their feet' (Hebrews 2:7–8; see Psalm 8:5–6); 'You are the salt of the earth' and 'the light of the world. A city set on a hill cannot be hidden' (Matthew 5:13a, 14). As Jesus' followers we must come out into the open, be proud of what we achieve with the gifts we have been given and do all we can to be distinctive lights in our secular environment. With lives based on these biblical truths, our self-esteem will surely be enriched.

Precious to God

There are many references in the Bible to precious stones. When the law was given and the use of the tabernacle in worship defined, the robes to be worn by the high priest were vividly described (Exodus 28). His breastplate was crafted with twelve precious stones representing the twelve sons (and tribes) of Israel, each bearing the name of one son. The high priest alone entered the holy of holies and came into God's presence, wearing the breastplate. This symbolism is powerful: we too are beautifully crafted by God, and now Jesus as our High Priest in heaven carries each individual in his heart; each one of us is loved by him and precious to him.

George's story (part 2)

When George opened that chapel door, a fresh understanding awaited him—one of love and acceptance. He found within the chapel a small group of Christians praying. He was about to run away when someone who knew him beckoned him to sit down. It was with some hesitancy that he did so. As the story of his pain unfolded later that evening, he felt listened to and understood. Through this encounter, he decided not to leave after all and he was drawn into the fellowship of Christians within his college. He began to explore Christianity in some depth and just three months later he professed publicly his faith in Jesus through confirmation.

This is not the end of the story. George had to find out he was precious to God and others, and it was Christian people who helped him towards that awareness in the way they accepted him, listened to him and cared for him. He began to develop healthy and well-grounded self-esteem; the love he received from God and others enabled him to begin to love himself. Gradually he began to live and behave differently.

It is easy to confuse humility with low self-esteem, but Paul reminds us that 'he [Jesus] humbled himself and became obedient to death—even death on the cross' (Philippians 2:8). Biblical humility is a total willingness to submit to God's will. God has set us an example in Jesus, who was 'humble and gentle in heart' (Matthew 11:29). Jesus himself invites us to be yoked with him and find rest for our souls. Through being yoked to Jesus, our burdens are shared and we can walk in step with our maker and provider and know intimately how he values and loves us. Here humility and healthy self-esteem can go hand in hand.

Paul characterises the life worthy of our calling by telling the Ephesians, 'Be completely humble and gentle; be patient, bearing with one another in love' (Ephesians 4:1–2). John Stott interprets the word *tapeinotes* (lowliness of mind) as 'the humble recognition of the worth and value of other people, the humble mind that was in Christ and led him to empty himself and become a servant'.[1] Paradoxically, developing this kind of humility is one of the ways in which our masks of low self-esteem can be lifted so that we can start to live life in all its fullness.

Prayer for those struggling with low self-esteem

O God, I am not one of those omni-competent people and so I have little to offer others. Help me to be willing to believe that you see me as precious and unique. Help me to be willing to believe others when they praise and encourage me. Help me to believe that I am someone of worth in my own right and do not need to compare myself with anyone else.

Suggestions

- Jesus affirms Zacchaeus, the tax collector, by singling him out from the crowd and inviting himself to his home (Luke 19:5). Find other examples from Jesus' ministry of outcasts whom he affirms through his acceptance of them and in each case describe how the person's life is changed.
- Are there individuals within your church who seem to need encouragement and friendship? Consider ways in which you and others could show God's love to them, affirming them and involving them in the fellowship and life of the church.

- If you suffer from low self-esteem, list the ways in which this affects you in your everyday life. Share these with a trusted friend.
- What have you learned from this chapter that will help you to value yourself more? Consider any action you would like to take. Write this down and refer to it from time to time.
- John 17:13–16 makes it clear to us as Christians that we are in the world but not of the world. What does this mean and does it have a bearing on how you understand healthy self-esteem?
- Spend time reflecting on your own good qualities. You could thank God for these and share your thoughts and feelings with a friend.
- In twos (or more) reflect back the other person's successes, good actions, admirable qualities and so on.

Chapter 2

Depression: not alone

Even though I walk through the valley of the shadow of death, I will fear no evil, for you are with me; your rod and your staff, they comfort me.

PSALM 23:4

When the darkness comes I remember truth discovered in the light, and hang on to this with everything I've got.[2]

Depression has many guises. My own experience was one of feeling that the bottom had dropped out of my life, leaving me with a huge gaping hole of emptiness and isolation. Although I was going through the motions of living, even dragging myself to work each day, I felt life was totally without meaning and enjoyment. There was no glimmer of light or hope ahead and no escape. These feelings came over me gradually and stayed with me for a very long time quite different from the feeling I have now of being a bit 'down in the dumps', which is normally short-lived. Sir Winston Churchill, who suffered from depression, called his condition the 'black dog'. Matthew Johnstone, a sufferer of depression himself, in his book *Living with a Black Dog*, examines, explains and demystifies one of the most widespread and debilitating problems afflicting modern society, using simple text and illustrations.[3]

My story

I sank into depression without realising it. Three years previously I had suffered a shattering bereavement of the person I was to marry. As I struggled so hard to come to terms with this loss, I became angry with God for allowing the death to happen. What I was experiencing didn't seem real; I was carrying on with life in a kind of vacuum and on automatic pilot. However, reality did gradually begin to set in and with it the pain of the prospect of unending separation; I felt that I could no longer journey through life on my own; an excruciating 'aloneness' lay ahead. I began to withdraw into my shell, unable to interact with others, unable to share the pain, becoming distant even from those closest and dearest to me. I had left God out of it all and didn't call for his help.

However, I did have one dear friend and colleague—I was teaching at the time—who understood something of what I was going through. Unfortunately I was unable to talk about my feelings or what had happened, but nevertheless the whole situation (which I had 'swept under the carpet') began to surface. One Saturday my friend found me in my apartment almost paralysed with grief; I shall never forget her compassion and understanding. Wisely she encouraged me to seek help and I realised that I could no longer hide my grief from my family, friends and colleagues. I was locked into a state of depression, with the stigma that goes with it, and in a place from which I wanted to run a thousand miles. With the help and support of a psychiatrist and with medication, I was given some breathing space, but the depression scarcely lifted. With the benefit of hindsight I realised that my emotions—the pain and buried grief—needed to be shared.

My psychiatrist may well have seen me as a suicide risk and was wise to suggest that if ever I felt desperate I was to phone him. One Friday evening I did just that and within a couple of hours I was admitted into what was called a 'neurosis unit' within a psychiatric hospital. Funded by the state, patients with professional backgrounds were selected for this particular unit where the stay was normally limited to two or three months. Treatment took the form mainly of antidepressants with group and art therapy. One of my happier memories was working together with a BBC reporter to produce the unit's weekly newspaper. My self-esteem went shooting up! The saddest memory was the suicide of another person within our group. Slowly with medication and various therapies I came out of my depression, returning home within a few weeks, better equipped to lead a more fulfilling and satisfying life within God's love and tender care.

I have learned so much from this traumatic episode of depression and I look back with gratitude to my friends and my family who were alongside me at the time, praying for me and visiting me in that psychiatric unit. Over subsequent years I have had the opportunity to accompany and encourage others with depression along their paths to recovery.

I tell my story with reluctance but trusting that its message may be of help to those who stoically say 'I'm fine!' and try to hide the depression and its associated baggage, as I did.

Facts about mental health in the UK

- Around 300 people out of 1,000 will experience mental health problems every year in Britain.
- 230 will visit a GP.
- 102 of these will be diagnosed with a mental health problem, mainly depression.
- 24 will be referred to a specialist psychiatric service.
- 6 per cent will become in-patients in psychiatric hospitals.
- About half of people with common mental health problems are no longer affected after 18 months. Poorer people, the long-term sick and unemployed people are more likely to be longer affected than the general population.

Self-harm statistics show the UK to have one of the highest rates in Europe and suicides, especially among men, were on the increase in 2011 and 2012. In reality men are just as likely to experience depression as women but are less likely to seek help. Just as men often find it difficult to open the window of their car and ask for directions, so too they are reluctant to seek help when depressed and are often unable to recognise how serious their symptoms are. Men in particular often display anger and aggression in their depression, to which others may not react kindly or with understanding. Crying and other signs of weakness have traditionally been frowned on in our culture as far as men are concerned; for women, crying is much more acceptable and this is therapeutic as it communicates sadness and the need for help. Unfortunately a small minority of men in particular leave it too late to go for help and, finding themselves totally unable to cope and seeing no escape route, take their own lives. I know of one such situation. This spells out the seriousness of hiding these symptoms from others and delaying going to the GP for help.

Symptoms of depression

For those suffering from depression a number of symptoms may be evident, such as:

- feelings of worthlessness and guilt
- sleeping difficulties: either too little or too much
- poor or increased appetite
- a sad, dejected or moody frame of mind
- difficulty in communicating
- strained relationships
- difficulty in concentrating and making decisions
- recurring thoughts of helplessness and suicide
- the outside world seeming unimportant
- physical symptoms such as headaches and palpitations
- feelings of darkness and being in a tunnel
- loss of interest in almost all usual activities and in sex
- tiredness and exhaustion
- anger and aggression, especially in men.

Additional symptoms for Christians may include:

- little interest in reading the Bible
- no joy in life
- difficulty with prayer

- feeling remote from God
- feelings of guilt
- no desire to attend church or meet with other Christians.

Experiencing two or three of these symptoms for a short time due to particularly difficult circumstances may not necessarily indicate that someone has clinical depression.

However, when these symptoms don't go away, help is needed for diagnosis and if necessary for treatment so that the depression doesn't become any more severe. With the benefit of hindsight, had I sought help sooner my depression would have been far less serious. We are well aware that if we develop a bronchial infection it is common sense to go to the GP to prevent the condition deteriorating. However, when we have a mental disorder such as depression, we tend to be reluctant to seek professional help, hindered by the stigma associated with this condition, and we are more likely to struggle on without support or relief.

I know of a pastor who was obviously depressed. When encouraged by a friend to see his GP, he did so reluctantly and, at the last minute in the surgery, he chickened out, deciding to complain about heart pains and not about what was going on inside his heart and mind. He was referred to a cardiologist and his condition of depression remained undisclosed and untreated until its severity resulted in a breakdown.

Causes of depression

Upbringing

Depression in adulthood is often due to childhood experiences and upbringing. Unstable homes deprived of love and security, parents splitting up, bullying at school and broken friendships can all play a part. Then there are those whose parents had unrealistic expectations for their children's achievements, especially academically. A child can end up feeling enormous pressure not to be a disappointment to their parents. Today youngsters have increasing opportunities to develop their talents in areas such as music, art and drama. Instead of being able to enjoy these activities for what they are, children start to be pressurised to pass exams and it all becomes a drudgery. Sometimes parental ambitions can be achieved at too high a cost, with the children vulnerable to depression either at the time or later in life.

Jack's story

Jack has suffered from bi-polar depression since his teenage years. He is intelligent but endured much suffering during his childhood at the hands of a dominant and controlling father who put him under enormous pressure to achieve and succeed. He did do well at school, gaining a place at Cambridge, only to opt out after his first year; to the disappointment of his father, his sole success had been on the cricket field, and he was asked by his college to curtail his studies and leave. After this, his father regarded him as a complete failure. Jack decided that the pressure of trying to please his father was too great, so he severed links with him and went his own way in life. However, the standards set during those early formative years were so ingrained in him that he began to believe that anything he did that was less than perfect was unacceptable; this mindset had a seriously damaging effect on him both mentally and emotionally.

So, needing from time to time to protect himself from the everyday stresses of life, he had episodes when he withdrew into his shell, spending much of the working day in bed, sinking deep into depression, each episode often lasting for several weeks. He would then emerge and enjoy a period of relative normality for several months until his suppressed emotions would resurface. There would then be periods of elation when he saw the world as his oyster and he would devise intricate, reasoned, but unrealistic plans for his future which no one dared to thwart.

The peaks and valleys experienced in bipolarity can severely damage relationships. Many gifted people, including Stephen Fry, actor, comedian, presenter and writer, suffer from the condition.

In his award-winning documentary *Stephen Fry: The Secret Life of the Manic Depressive*, he openly shares his experiences of living with the disorder and interviews a number of celebrities who also suffer from it. In recent years there has been more understanding about the causes of this illness, with great strides being made in its treatment.

Illness

Illness, surgery and accidents can play a part in the onset of the disorder. It is not uncommon, for instance, after surgery or after diagnosis leading to surgery for someone to develop depression, affecting their decision-making and day-to-day living. With the intense focus on the illness itself and the person generally feeling out of sorts, the depression may not be recognised and hence go undiagnosed. Diseases of the nervous system, such as Parkinson's disease and multiple sclerosis, are known to be accompanied by depression.

People with dementia have an increased risk of suffering from depression. The difficulty these people may have in communicating their distress and the fact that the symptoms are hidden within the dementia may mean that the depression can be missed and remain untreated. With elderly people, loss of interaction with and interest in others, combined with a feeling of gloominess, may indicate the onset of a depressive illness.

Loss and trauma

Depression can be caused by particular stressful events in our lives. Trauma, redundancy, the birth of a child, relationship breakdown, loss and loneliness are potential triggers. I can see that my own depression was the result of the suppression of emotions after loss; for others depression might arise out of suppressed anger or circumstances. I know of an 80-year-old woman who fell and broke her arm for the second time in the same year. She was angry about this and also about becoming old and vulnerable. However, she suppressed these emotions for fear of upsetting her family; as a result, she gradually sank into a state of depression which could have been avoided.

Physiological and physical factors
Depression has physical implications which can include chemical imbalance in the brain. People who have a predisposition towards the condition can have anxious personalities or suffer from low self-esteem. When confronted by external pressures they may find difficulty in coping and this can be a recurring pattern in their lives. Lack of sleep can be a symptom or be among the causes, as can lack of exercise or an unhealthy diet.

Loneliness
It's not surprising that those who are cut off from others, feeling lonely and unloved, hiding their sorrow behind their masks, can become victims of depression. The next chapter addresses ways in which we can help ourselves or others with feelings of isolation and thus prevent the onset of depression.

Alcohol and drugs
All too often, when people can't cope they turn to alcohol or drugs. They are under the illusion that these will make them feel better, but that 'feeling better' is likely to be short-lived. Alcohol itself can cause depression, so it is crucial to guard against over-dependence on it.

The Christian and depression

No Christian is immune to depression. In fact I believe that Christians may be more susceptible to it, having a greater awareness of their flawed nature and their constant striving for Christlikeness. Some Christians regard depression as a weakness and even a sin and consequently feel ashamed when they can't shake it off. They tend to adopt a stoical approach, determined to hide the symptoms from others and just grin and bear it.

A refusal to go for help may result from thoughts such as: I don't want to be judged; it's a sin to be depressed; I need to work it out alone with God; I feel frightened, ashamed and guilty; I don't trust anyone to keep to themselves what I say; I'll sort myself out on my own. Such mindsets can make people withdraw more deeply into their shell and cause their pain to become more intense. The message we have to convey is that there is nothing shameful in depression—most people experience it at some stage in their lives—but no one needs to be its slave, for help is at hand.

Another reason why a Christian may refuse to go for help is illustrated in the story below.

Elizabeth's story

Elizabeth is married with three young children and has been prone to depression most of her life. Each time she falls into a depressive state, she sees it as a spiritual battle to be won through faith and prayer. She takes herself on a retreat and battles it out, on her own with God. Her depression has all the hallmarks of clinical depression—an imbalance in her brain—but she prefers not to go for professional help.

Elizabeth is one among many who blame themselves for their depression, seeing it not as an illness but as the deliberate work of the devil in their lives, from which they need to battle to be released.

Effects of depression

Negative feelings and thoughts

We have seen in the previous chapter how negative feelings about ourselves and our achievements can cause depression. It is easy to understand, too, how failure, wrongdoing and guilt can lead along that same path, especially when the person is unwilling to disclose to others what has occurred.

Alan's story (part 1)

Alan loved his work as a youth leader in his church and felt much more fulfilled than he had done as a teacher. He had a young family to support, so at certain times he supplemented his income by giving private tuition in his subject, physics. He was paid in cash and failed to declare this on his tax return. When he saw the gravity of what he was guilty of—fraud—he was mortified. He had always had high moral standards and instilled those same standards in his children, as well as the youngsters he served in church. His guilt was enormous and he was too ashamed to tell anyone. He could not get the situation out of his mind; it went round and round in his head, especially in bed at night. During the day he felt crushed by an enormous weight from which he couldn't escape. The guilt and failure became a mindset. It was apparent that he was depressed and needed help. Instead, he saw himself as no good and handed in his notice at the church.

Alan's negative feelings and thoughts were made worse by the fact that he had to face up to the cultural stigma of his illness. When I was suffering from depression, I found it difficult to accept the fact that it was actually an illness; I felt a fraud and assumed others saw me in this light. I probably came across as a misery who ought to be told to 'pull yourself together and enjoy life'. The very nature of the illness doesn't allow enjoyment, but, though I longed for others to understand how I felt, it was too scary to come out into the open; I didn't want to risk being perceived as mentally ill. We may be just emerging from a society that tends to stigmatise illnesses of the mind; in my own depression I found it difficult to accept that I was not responsible for my mental state. Without medical help I would have been unlikely to get better.

Family and friends

Most of the symptoms experienced in depression can have a profound effect on family and friends. Depressed people tend to retreat from others, wanting to curl up and be alone; they may withdraw from the intimacy of physical contact and interaction. I know of one depressed person who, although close to her family, was unable to share her feelings with any of them.

How the church can help

Having looked briefly at the causes and the effects of depression, how can we, in the church, help one another?

Getting real

Those Christians who, like Elizabeth, consider it a sin and weakness to suffer from depression may have to face up to the reality that God doesn't always answer their prayers in the way they anticipate. Paul had to face up to unanswered prayer in his own life in relation to the 'thorn in the flesh' from which he suffered: 'Three times I pleaded with God to take it away from me' (2 Corinthians 12:8). He prayed with total confidence for release but that was not given to him and he probably had to live with this weakness for the rest of his life. However, as we read in verse 9, acceptance enabled Paul to experience God's grace and strength: 'My grace is sufficient for you, for my power is made perfect in weakness.'

Encouraging a person to acknowledge that they have a problem and that it isn't wrong to feel depressed is the first priority. To understand that God wants us to be 'whole' people and to enjoy life in all its fullness may give them the motivation to come out into the open and seek help. God is the ultimate healer, so prayer is essential in the healing process. The sufferer him/herself may find difficulty in praying; for them to be told that you are praying for them can be very consoling. Our role as fellow Christians is obviously to pray, but also to help and encourage the sufferer to take some kind of action by gently communicating that God heals through professionals whom he equips for his purposes.

Offering friendship

God created us to be in relationship with others. In the New Testament, many of Paul's letters begin and end with tributes to his friends, those who ministered to him, supported him, prayed for him and loved him. At the close of Acts 20, Luke writes a moving account of Paul's farewell to his close friends in Ephesus as he sets sail towards Jerusalem.

Friends are those who accept us as we are and do not judge us. In times of depression it can make all the difference to have a trusted friend around who can draw alongside and listen to the pain.

Listening

Those who have the gift of listening can play a valuable role in the depressed person's recovery. It is very powerful to be genuinely listened to, helping us to feel loved, understood and accepted. For those who find concentrated listening difficult, I would recommend a basic course in listening skills such as that offered by the Acorn Christian Healing Foundation. This organisation also has available Christians trained in listening skills who can help those who would prefer to share with someone not personally known to them, or who do not know of anyone within their church with whom they would feel comfortable talking. The church might well help the depressed person to explore this avenue of help.

How people can help themselves

To those who are willing to take some kind of action, I want to suggest three avenues of practical help.

GPs

Ideally the GP should be the depressed person's first port of call. Someone I know plucked up courage to see his doctor about his depressed state and asked the receptionist for a double appointment, as he knew ten minutes or so would be insufficient time to offload his burden and talk through how he could be helped. Some

GPs are excellent and skilled in diagnosis and treatment. However others are not, and if this is the case, or the relationship with the GP is a bit strained, to ask for referral to a psychiatrist or counsellor might be a wise option.

Counselling

To have a friend in place who is skilled in listening and who will pray may be the first step on the way to recovery, but professional therapies such as counselling should also be considered. In the UK the Association of Christian Counsellors has an online database and this can help people to find a qualified Christian counsellor in their area (see Resources, p. 176). Counsellors are able to give support and the opportunity to explore and gain insights into what is actually going on in someone's life.

Medication

There are many different types of antidepressants available which help to change the chemical imbalance in the brain. If a course of these is recommended by a medical professional, it would be wise not to refuse. The medication can take two or three weeks to kick in but it can make a big difference. It is not uncommon for GPs or psychiatrists to recommend both medication and a talking therapy.

Changing a mindset

With help, people can learn to develop new and healthier mindsets. Alan felt guilty because he had done wrong. The right way to deal with guilt feelings is to put things right and receive forgiveness. The wrong way to deal with it is to carry on feeling worse and worse and develop a mindset that tells us we are bad and worthless—end of story. Christians have the wonderful resource of God's forgiveness, as they acknowledge what they have done wrong and that they want to deal with it. We have an example of this outworking in the life of Peter, who denied Jesus three times (Luke 22:54–60). This denial gave way to remorse and he went outside and wept bitterly (vv. 61–62). But he later received Jesus' forgiveness and restoration (John 21:15–17).

It's worth adding that there are people who develop a mindset of guilt although they have done nothing wrong. They need to be reassured and encouraged by others and to know God's acceptance of them and his love.

Alan's story (part 2)

Alan had suffered from depression since he was a teenager but the condition became much more severe as he grew older. Previously he had been able to hide it or seemed to get over it but this time he couldn't shake it off. The effects on his wife and family were devastating: his wife couldn't believe it when he gave up his work. Alan's vicar, too, was mystified by his letter of resignation and he immediately went round to see him, for he realised that something had to be seriously wrong. Alan was an outstanding youth leader and the youngsters loved him. It became obvious to the vicar that Alan was depressed; he was having difficulty in communicating, had lost weight and was looking far from well. His wife filled in some of those details and the vicar then acted promptly. First, he encouraged Alan to see his doctor, stressing to him that depression was an illness and nothing to be ashamed of and suggesting that the doctor would be able to help. Secondly, very sensitively, he tried to tease out of Alan what had happened to trigger the depression.

Off-loading his guilt was the first step on Alan's road to recovery. He was given medication by his GP and then put in touch with a local Christian counsellor. Here he was able again to share his feelings of guilt and also for the first time to talk about his previous bouts of depression. To know that God was still there for him and that he could claim complete forgiveness and wipe the slate clean was truly liberating for him. The Inland Revenue was having an amnesty at the time to encourage people to come out into the open about their tax evasion and with the support of a church leader he was able to sort out the problem that was troubling him and that had triggered the depression. Within three months he was back at work with fresh vigour and enthusiasm.

Learning to be more outgoing

As we have seen, when a person is depressed, they want to withdraw from social contact and probably avoid going to church. This is all very understandable, but what a difference it can make when the depressed person makes an effort to meet with others. Going to church and/or belonging to a group who share the same interests can be the means of helping us to make friends, develop more social skills and be more outgoing. This may be hard but, with help from trusted friends, not impossible. For such friends to continue to keep in touch may even help to guard against the onset of depression in the future.

How God and the Bible can help

Depression is not mentioned as such in the Bible, although there are more than a hundred references to distress and half that number mention anguish.

One biblical story worth reading in full and reflecting on is that of Elijah in 1 Kings 19. Following his victory on Mount Carmel against the prophets of Baal, Queen Jezebel threatened murder, which prompted a fearful Elijah to flee into the wilderness and sit alone under a solitary broom tree, plunging into a state of despondency and wanting to die. 'I have had enough, Lord,' he said. 'Take my life; I am no better than my ancestors' (v. 4). Totally overwhelmed by fear and failure, he found relief from his trauma in sleep. But God didn't give up on him and his life wasn't taken. As the story unfolds, we see Elijah gently nurtured and reassured of God's presence. He had a dialogue with God and was helped to understand that he was wrong to think he was the only prophet who had remained faithful to the true God. He was then given a simple task to do. Finally God gave him a companion in Elisha and he was able to resume his ministry. What a lot we can learn through this story about helping someone with depression! God didn't get angry or condemn Elijah but drew alongside him, providing the therapy he needed.

Another story in the Old Testament in which despair follows victory is that of Samson. We see him emotionally and physically drained, vulnerable and full of self-pity. He was thirsty and cried out angrily to God, '"You have given your servant this great victory. Must I now die of thirst and fall into the hands of the uncircumcised?" Then God opened up the hollow place in Lehi, and water came out of it. When Samson drank, his strength returned and he revived' (Judges 15:18–19a). We can feel drained and be at our most vulnerable after successes in life but, although it may be hard to believe at the time, God is there to nurture and sustain us and out of weakness bring us strength. As we draw near to others to share the pain, so we can draw close to God himself, who is our ultimate healer.

I would not want to suggest that Elijah or Samson had chronic depression, but I think we can learn something from these stories and others. Some people are helped through turning to the Bible and reflecting on God's goodness to his people. As already mentioned, I personally receive comfort and encouragement from the psalms, for they reflect the wide spectrum of human experience. I can identify with the psalmists in their struggles with life's pain and problems, as they try to talk and 'listen' to God. In Psalm 42 the psalmist longs for the past days, when he 'used to go with the multitude leading the procession to the house of God, with shouts of joy among the festive throng' (v. 4). 'My soul thirsts for God' (v. 2), he cries, yearning once again to lead the procession to the temple in Jerusalem, where God's presence was intensely real. The psalmist seems at the time to be living far away to the north of Jerusalem in the beautiful area of Mount Carmel. We are not told in the psalm why he is unable to return to Jerusalem, God's home, but we are aware that he feels cut off from God.

'Even though I walk through the valley of the shadow of death, I will fear no evil, for you are with me; your rod and your staff, they comfort me' (Psalm 23:4). The words of David's psalm, known and loved by so many, are a vivid reminder of God's love, presence and protection through all life's troubles.

Over the years I have led a number of groups to the Holy Land and one of the many highlights for me is to take the old road from Jerusalem to Jericho, named Wadi Kelt—a truly dramatic setting both for this psalm and for the parable of the good Samaritan. Drivers are often reluctant to take parties along this stony old track, preferring the safer, quicker tarmac road. However, when a driver has given in to persuasion, our group has penetrated into the depths of the uninviting deep gorge with its sharp bends and high cliffs. For David this valley was a picture of depression, yet he knew God's presence within it. Although the valley, as I recall it, seems to go on for ever, it does end when Jericho comes into view, reflecting the thought that there is light through the tunnel of depression as well.

An episode of depression can be a shattering experience. As Christians we have committed and entrusted our lives to God. Nothing has changed: he is still there with us and, even if perhaps we don't feel it, we must continue to put our trust in him. We still belong to God, so let us not lose out by abandoning our faith but instead rest in his promise, 'Never will I leave you; never will I forsake you' (Hebrews 13:5). As we acknowledge God as our ultimate healer, let us put our hand in his through the tunnel of depression and on into his eternal light. Here is a prayer that you may like to make your own:

Prayer for those struggling with depression and also those supporting them

Dear God our Father, thank you for being our refuge and strength in good times and bad. Thank you that, although we may not feel your presence, we can rest in your promise that you will never leave us nor forsake us. In your infinite mercy, we pray that you will bring peace and comfort to those of us who sometimes face days filled with the pain of depression. We pray that you will walk before and beside us in our journey on this earth. Bring to us friends in our dark times to love and support us. Help us not to forget the blessings of the past and through these enable us to trust you for the future. Amen

Suggestions

- Physical fitness helps all of us to be mentally healthy and alert and can play a strategic role in the lives of depressed people and those prone to depression. With one or two others, you could work out ways of improving your physical fitness through exercise and diet.
- If you know nothing about depression, how about looking at the Bibliography at the end of this book and choosing a title to give you some information about it?
- If you are suffering from depression or emerging from it, how about setting yourself a small daily task rather than expecting too much of yourself?
- It may be wise not to listen to too much news. If you do, focus on the more cheerful happenings—if there are any!
- Buy an attractive notebook and keep a journal of your feelings each day.
- Try to do something at least once a week that you enjoy, such as gardening or going with a friend on a country walk or out to tea or a film.
- If you are finding it difficult to go to church, consider arriving late and leaving early, as a starter, preferably asking a friend to go with you.
- Reflect on the psalms and try to find one in which the thoughts and emotions of the psalmist are similar to yours. Use this for comfort and prayer.

Chapter 3

Loneliness: finding acceptance and friendship

God sets the lonely in families.

PSALM 68:6

Loneliness is an inner emptiness with both a fear of and a longing for close relationships with others.

I am sure that many of us have experienced loneliness at some period in our lives and will be able to identify with one or more of the stories in this chapter. Andrew craved for company and hoped to find this within his church.

Andrew's story (part 1)

Andrew stood sipping a cup of coffee in the church foyer after the morning service. If only the coffee had been a glass of wine, he might have felt more relaxed and less sensitive to what was going on around him. It was lonely for him in this environment with cliques of people standing around in groups, chatting about what they had been doing and making plans to meet up for this and that during the coming week. He had shaken hands with the vicar, who had enquired how he was doing, to which he replied that he was fine! He knew that this was far from the truth. He longed to share with someone the anguish that was going on in his life: the fact that he had lost his job and had little prospect of finding another; that his father, who had had great expectations for him, no longer seemed to want contact with him; that God now played little part in his life and that the sermon he had just heard had little meaning for him in his current circumstances. Behind the mask he showed to the outside world hid a lonely man feeling unloved, worthless and helpless.

Andrew was shy and had always envied the social skills and ease with which others were able to converse. Since he had left university twelve years previously, he had buried himself in his work as a pharmaceutical research chemist. His father had wanted him to follow in his own footsteps by becoming a vet, but a vocational psychologist had suggested that research was a career more suited to his introverted personality. He had enjoyed his work and saw himself as having been quite successful in what he had achieved. Then quite suddenly funding had run out and overnight he had been made redundant.

He didn't want others to see that he was alone and something of a misfit and in any case no one seemed to want to talk with him, so he moved across to the welcome desk. No one was there to give a welcome, so, after giving a fleeting glance at the information displayed about church activities, he slipped out of the side door and into the car park. He breathed a sigh of relief that he could now step back into the comfort of his own world. He vowed he would not go to church again—it was all too painful. He had no job, no friends, no one who cared about him or who needed him, no one who would miss him. What could he do to alleviate all this? He could drive his car into a wall and that would be it. Mercifully, reason kicked in and he chose to drown his sorrows in a bottle of wine.

Today's culture of accelerating technological development is in danger of increasing loneliness across our society, not least among those who are spending more time on their computers than in the company of others. It is great to be able to use modern technology in our churches to produce beautiful magazines and notices, having a website and so on, but we should take care that we don't end up technology-focused rather than people-centred. A well-ordered welcome desk with details of church meetings and activities is fine, but if there is no one there to give the welcome or to talk to, something is very wrong.

What is loneliness?

Loneliness is not the same as being alone or experiencing solitude. You can be alone and yet not feel lonely. Although Andrew was among a lot of people at the end of the service, he felt intensely lonely; he needed to talk, but no one seemed at all interested in him.

Solitude, on the other hand, is quite different, for it is a voluntary choice and often the means through which a Christian's relationship with God is deepened and spiritual growth enhanced. Jesus was led by the Holy Spirit into the wilderness, alone, to be spiritually tested (Matthew 4:1). Following the miracle of the feeding of the 5000, he sent the disciples on ahead and dismissed the crowd, and then 'he went up on a mountainside by himself to pray' (Matthew 14:23). There are references to other occasions when Jesus retreated for solitude and prayer. Seeking solitude was an important priority for him.

I am writing this chapter in a charming rural retreat centre in East Sussex (see Resources, p. 176). I need to be alone for this task but I don't feel lonely. One or two people are here for fasting and prayer—a combination of practices which I must one day explore. For me, at the moment, the food here is too good to miss!

It is difficult to put into words the exact feeling of loneliness. The experience is different for each individual and reactions to similar circumstances can vary enormously. As with all feelings, we cannot say, for instance, that we know *exactly* how Andrew felt. Some people would describe loneliness as an inner emptiness with both a fear of and a longing for close relationships with others; all this can be accompanied by fear of facing the future alone. Some Christians experience spiritual loneliness when perhaps through circumstances they feel cut off from God, although in theory they *know* that he will not leave or forsake them. All such thoughts and feelings can be hidden behind a mask of 'normality' because to admit to being lonely can be admitting to feelings of weakness and inadequacy. From early infancy anyone can be a sufferer and most of us have experienced a measure of loneliness at some stage in life. Whatever your age, whether or not you personally are a victim of loneliness or know someone who is, I invite you to come on a voyage of discovery towards greater understanding of the causes of loneliness and its effects and to find ways to remove the mask and start to make meaningful relationships.

Causes of loneliness

Life events

Circumstances can be a contributing factor to feelings of loneliness. I recall that when my husband left me, I felt agonisingly lonely. There was no one around to bring me a cup of tea in the morning. I felt that no one needed me or wanted me.

Change of any kind can bring in its wake loneliness and insecurity: those who have been rejected or widowed, moved house or changed church or workplace, taken retirement or, like Andrew, been made redundant often experience them. Life continues to evolve, and if we resist its inevitable movement in our own fractured lives, we may well spiral down into disorder, insecurity and loneliness.

Children can suffer the agony of loneliness and still hide its pain. I can recall our family moving when I was just nine. I had to start a new school in mid-term and join a class of eleven-year-olds who treated me very unkindly. Having made no friends, break times were agony for me as I felt totally excluded. What's more, one of my classmates began to tease and bully me. I tried to put on a brave face until the day came when I could bear it no longer. I told our teacher that I felt ill and I was taken to the medical room. It was a great relief to be able to cry openly without the fear of being mocked by my classmates. I kept up the pretence of feeling ill but I suspect that others were aware of the bullying that was going on.

It warms my heart to see parents encouraging their own children to look out in the school playground for those on their own and include them in their games and activities. Even at a young age they can learn to develop feelings of empathy for others who are lonely and invite them into their homes, perhaps even suggesting that they join them for Sunday school or a church activity.

Old age

Older people, through failing health, immobility, bereavement, the death of friends, loss of purpose and boredom, can experience acute feelings of loneliness, which they may often try to hide from others. As illustrated in the following stories, some are able to develop a philosophical and positive attitude of mind towards ageing but for many this is not so easy.

Mary's and David's stories

Mary is 98, unmarried, and over many decades has been a real pillar of the church. She has been a very caring person and has already left a legacy in others' lives, not least within families where she has been a regular baby-sitter. With no family and having lost her close friend some years ago, she could have been lonely. However, she is much loved and hardly a Sunday passes without her being invited by a family for lunch. In learning to give and receive, she has found a rich pattern in life.

David, on the other hand, is not much more than 70. Shortly after his retirement from the police force at 60, sadly his wife died of a sudden heart attack. He used to be a regular churchgoer and over many years was involved in the youth group. Now he rarely attends church and spends much of his time watching television. When someone from the church visits him he comes across as a poor lonely old man. No one really knows what is going on behind his 'I'm fine, thank you!' attitude. With encouragement from others and his own willingness to open up and share his thoughts, it would be possible for him to be helped towards a better quality of life, but, whatever the reason, this doesn't seem to be happening.

The contrast between these two stories speaks for itself.

For those people who just cannot come to terms with their changed circumstances and are unable to find their way out of their loneliness, professional help may be worth exploring. This will mean removing the mask labelled 'I'm fine!', but the effort of doing so will be well worth it. People often resist change and choose the familiar, which, although miserable, is safe. It requires courage to emerge from what is known into unexplored territory. As Christians we are reminded that we have a God who tells us to be strong and courageous and who says, 'Never will I leave you; never will I forsake you' (Hebrews 13:5).

Nature and nurture
We are shaped by nature and nurture: low self-esteem, shyness and introverted personalities can be inhibiters in social situations and barriers to the making of friendships. Youngsters with physical or intellectual disabilities can suffer acute feelings of loneliness and exclusion, although it is hoped that following the 2012 Paralympic Games there will be a lasting change of attitude so that people with disabilities are treated by others as of equal worth. Those working in psychiatric hospitals, in care homes or with dysfunctional families see loneliness as one of the common traits in those for whom they care.

Work
Some church leaders are reluctant to make personal friendships within their congregation and this can cause loneliness. Whether or not this is the case, most will be carrying confidentialities which they are unable to share, and when there are difficult issues to resolve and they are unable to find a reliable and suitable mentor or adviser to whom they can refer they can feel quite isolated.

Christian witness
I personally would not relish the prospect of being a lone Christian within the workplace or classroom. This is all too common these days as the Christian faith becomes increasingly marginalised. Since

God created us as relational beings, the absence of companionship and affinity with others—over, for instance, ethical issues—can be very discouraging. Some fear ridicule and rejection so much that they prefer to hide their Christian beliefs from others. They would rather go with the crowd and keep their faith private. However, there are those who come out into the open about their Christian beliefs and in so doing become vulnerable to exclusion and loneliness. It takes courage to make such a stand and admit to being a follower of Jesus, not knowing initially what the reaction might be from colleagues and peers.

Deprivation

We may be only too aware of young people within our local communities who are lonely, unwanted and unloved. Many have no one within the home to whom to turn for help and support. Prospects of work may be limited. If we recall the riots in the summer of 2011 and the subsequent reports, we know that in many cases the rioting behaviour could ultimately be ascribed to poor parenting. In the misery of their loneliness and lack of love, young people may resort to violence, sexual promiscuity, drugs and alcohol. We talk about unwanted teenage pregnancies, but often the teenager, in her search for love, longs for a child to meet her basic needs of love and company. Churches normally care well for the children of their own members but can fail to reach vulnerable young people in the wider community. Within my own town, Churches Together have formed a Youth Trust which currently employs two youth workers who work tirelessly to befriend young people, drawing alongside them on their own territory.

Overprotection

In contrast, I am aware of youngsters who have had overprotective parents and been smothered by their love and attention; this we will see in Sarah's story. Becoming emotionally dependent on their parents for company and decision-making, they are not adequately equipped to face the outside world on their own. Consequently making and keeping meaningful friendships can be difficult and they can find themselves on the fringe of social life, feeling unaccepted and lonely.

Sarah's story

Sarah was educated at home by her mother, who wanted to protect her daughter from what she considered to be a corrupt culture. Sarah would accompany her parents to church each Sunday and go to Sunday school, and she quite enjoyed going along to the church youth club on Friday evenings but she didn't make any real friends there. Although she was seen as a bit of a misfit, she was treated kindly, but outside her home and church environment she rarely had the opportunity to make friends. Tragically, when Sarah was just 17, her mother suddenly developed an aggressive cancer and died just two months after the diagnosis.

Sarah's father was a quiet, submissive man who had not agreed with the way Sarah was brought up but did not intervene. However, Sarah's educational needs came to a head when the home situation radically changed. With just one year left before her education came to an end, the only alternative was to send Sarah to the local comprehensive, for which, not having attended school until then, she was not adequately equipped. Devoid of social skills and unable to relate to others in any meaningful way, Sarah found her life had become a misery; she missed her mother enormously, for she had depended on her and her protection so much. The loneliness Sarah experienced during those latter months of her education was agonising for her and continued into her adult life.

I have spoken to parents who, as they look back on the upbringing of their children, regret not giving them a greater degree of independence. They recall the way they 'mollycoddled' them and constantly worried about them. Much parental wisdom is needed in striking the right balance here, though without a doubt it is better to err on the side of love and protection than to be neglectful and unloving.

It is clear, then, that both neglect and overprotection of children can lead to feelings of insecurity and loneliness.

Effects of loneliness

Loneliness is a state from which most sufferers prefer to hide, rather than acknowledging it even to themselves.

Withdrawal

Some, like Andrew, will withdraw into self-centred isolation and opt for safety rather than risk reaching out and being open with others. Although they may come to church regularly, lonely people tend to disappear quickly at the end of the service for fear of being seen to be on their own. The effect of this can be that they live increasingly isolated and unstimulated lives.

Depression

Extreme loneliness can lead to depression, but, although the feelings associated with being depressed are unpleasant, people can receive the necessary professional help to move into a better place.

Loneliness can be the primary cause of suicide; when a person longs to be in relationship with others but feels that life is just too painful to endure alone, they may see suicide as the only escape route. Mercifully, a suicide attempt can be a cry for help and here a church that has a loving and caring fellowship can play a vital role in the healing and restoration process.

Workaholism

Others, hiding behind their masks of loneliness, bury themselves in work, as was the case with Andrew. Some workaholics can be so immersed in their job and ambitious lifestyle that they do not see the need for friends. Others may work long hours in order to mask their insecurities and prevent anyone from getting close enough to see what lies behind the mask.

Attention-seeking

In contrast, some lonely people may resort to exhibitionism and other attention-seeking devices as a way of 'crying' for help. The lonely person has low levels of self-esteem and self-confidence and consequently feels insecure. To counter these feelings they may create situations in which they become the centre of attention. For instance, some may feign a physical pain or illness and, with the temporary attention this creates, the feelings of inadequacies and loneliness are temporarily alleviated. Others may behave in a silly manner, talk loudly or blurt out inappropriate remarks.

Alcohol, drugs and pornography

Others may take refuge in alcohol, drugs or pornography to help dull the pain and end up becoming addicted to them.

Violence

In recent years the media have featured episodes of multiple killings and we may hear the perpetrators being described as 'loners'. We hear about neighbours who remark, 'He was very quiet and kept himself to himself. We would never have expected him to commit such an atrocity. We just can't believe it', perhaps indicating that the perpetrator couldn't control his frustrated loneliness and eventually expressed this through violence with tragic results. In some extreme cases, such violence may be a 'cry' for attention, a way of releasing the anger that people feel at their situation.

How the church can help

A church setting can actually accentuate loneliness if the members tend to congregate in cliques excluding others; this appears to have been the case in Andrew's church. We need to belong somewhere, so watching others in the 'in' group while we are 'outside' will be painful. Churches need to and can do better than this. We need to heed Paul's teaching in Romans 15:7: 'Accept one another... just as Christ accepted you.' Here was a diverse church of Jews and Gentiles being told to accept and welcome everyone. It is often through fellowship groups such as a home group where individuals are accepted, supported and nourished that the lonely can begin to shed their mask of loneliness as they begin to develop a sense of belonging. Jesus commands us to love God and our neighbours (Mark 12:30–31) and if we all did this well, no one would be lonely. This is the ideal which will only be fully realised in heaven. While we are still here on earth, however, we can help each other to build strong relationships with God and with other people.

This is easy to say but in reality those who have suffered loneliness over a considerable period and succumbed to feelings of isolation and to introspection may be reluctant to get involved. To invite such a person on their own or with another to our home or out for a cup of coffee could be a starting point. If that is not appropriate, we could arrange to accompany them to church or to a home group. A new person has joined a home group in our church recently and, although she has been attending services for a number of years, it has made all the difference to come to the home group with another member.

Andrew's story (part 2)

Late in the evening of that painful day when Andrew had tried to drink away his sorrows, his pastor, Tim, knocked at the door. At first Andrew didn't answer it, but when this was followed by a tap on the window he reluctantly opened the door and asked him in. Tim was able to listen to Andrew with such genuine warmth and compassion that he was encouraged to open up to him and admit his pain in feeling rejected through redundancy, as well as his feelings of loneliness within the church and his general sense of the meaninglessness of life. His mask was removed but only to Tim. However, that one person was able to point him lovingly and gently to Jesus, assuring him of his unconditional love and acceptance. Also, and very importantly, Andrew was gradually drawn into the hub of church life and shown the true love of Jesus through its members. He shed his mask of loneliness and experienced for the first time what it was to be a disciple and follower of Jesus Christ and to be part of the Christian family. Six months later he was given a voluntary job within a local charity and this led, a further six months later, with the help of glowing references from his manager and Tim, to his appointment as assistant manager in a local pharmacy. There he was valued as a person as well as for the skills he was able to offer.

How people can help themselves

God said that it is not good to be alone (Genesis 2:18). So, as well as enjoying our relationship with God, we all need to work out ways in which we can be in relationship with others. An individual has to be willing to admit that they are lonely, consider why this is so and try to do something to alleviate it. Sometimes they may need to accept the fact that the basic reason for the loneliness lies in themselves. They may suffer from low self-esteem and addressing this situation in a constructive way could help (see chapter 1).

Keep a diary

Some people find it helpful to keep a diary where they can write down their thoughts, behaviour and feelings and record particular occasions when they felt the pain of loneliness. This can then be analysed to help find the root cause; for example, the loneliness could be rooted in a fear of people and being rejected by them or in an inability to contribute to conversation in any meaningful way.

Seek professional help

Some people seek a professional counsellor or course to help them build up their confidence and self-esteem and acquire some social skills. If you are suffering from loneliness and find it hard to know how to go about this, try to make contact with a wise and trusted elder in the church and ask them to help you.

Andrew decided to give up church because its members had

let him down by not offering him the hand of friendship. It would have helped him to have taken the initiative in a conversation but lack of confidence, fear of rejection and his pain may well have prevented him from doing so.

Remember God's promises

'The Lord himself goes before and will be with you; he will never leave you nor forsake you' (Deuteronomy 31:8); this is one of many of God's amazing promises. To make a list of helpful and meaningful promises and then select one for the day could prove to be a helpful tool in times of loneliness.

How God and the Bible can help

As I write this chapter I am reminded of Jesus' encounter with Zacchaeus as told in Luke 19:1 9. This is a moving story about just one person who had the opportunity and privilege to meet Jesus during his earthly ministry. Zacchaeus was a chief tax collector, which means that he employed others to collect the taxes, passing on to the Romans what they required and probably keeping the rest for himself. He was rich, unpopular, shunned by many and, I suspect, lonely.

He perched himself up a sycamore tree, longing to get a good view of Jesus; he must have been totally stunned when Jesus looked up at him and commanded him to come down—for 'I must stay at your house today' (v. 5). Not in his wildest dreams did he imagine that Jesus would single him out in this way. He appeared to have no hesitation in responding, for we read that he came down at once. We are not told what was talked about in his house or who else was there, but we do have striking evidence of Jesus' impact on Zacchaeus, as he announced that he was giving half his gifts to the poor and recompensing those he had cheated. His life and relationships must have been transformed.

Jesus is with us today through his Holy Spirit. When we feel alone and deserted, with prayers seemingly unanswered, we need, as Zacchaeus did, to accept God's invitation and come to him just as we are. As we have communion with God who loves us and accepts us, we can learn to love and care for one another. God longs for us to develop a growing relationship with him—a true basis on which we can begin to counteract the problem of loneliness. As we share our innermost thoughts and desires with him, our masks of loneliness can drop away and our relationships with others can become satisfying and enriching.

Andrew stood by a welcome desk in church—lonely, excluded and needy—and nobody seemed to notice or care. Jesus noticed, though, and Andrew's needs and prayers were answered through the love and care of someone who finally did notice and care.

Prayer for those struggling with loneliness

O God, I feel so lonely at times. Please help me to find friendship and a place where I belong and feel accepted as I am. Please take away my fear of opening up to and trusting those who could help. Show me ways in which I can feel accepted and valued by others, by you and by myself. Amen

Suggestions

For those who are not lonely:

- Sit somewhere different in church.
- Talk casually, gently and in a friendly way to a new person.
- Get out of your usual clique of friends after a service.
- Look out for someone on their own, sit with them or talk with them after a service.
- Work out how best to offer hospitality. This could be for one person if you feel they may like to open up or for several as appropriate to help to bring others into a closer fellowship.

For those who are struggling with loneliness:

- Don't run away after a service unless you have to.
- If someone asks how you are and you feel they are genuine—someone you can trust—tell them honestly how you are feeling.
- Pluck up courage to join a group that shares an interest of yours or offers something to learn more about. Many people have found a new lease of life and developed new friendships through joining a choir, orchestra, gardening club, book club, historical society, arts club, voluntary organisation or something else. For those who have time during the day, the University of the Third Age (U3A) offers such opportunities and a group at a local level in many areas.

Chapter 4

Marriage issues: keeping love alive and growing

A man will leave his father and mother and be united to his wife, and the two will become one flesh.' This is a profound mystery.
EPHESIANS 5:31–32

Forgive and give as if it were your last opportunity. Love like there's no tomorrow, and if tomorrow comes, love again.[4]

In a short chapter such as this we can only just scratch the surface of the many reasons why marriages run into problems. As the victim of a broken marriage myself, I have a passion not just to save marriages but to protect and enhance this most precious of human relationships.

The Christian marriage commitment

Marriage is more than just a piece of paper; a Christian marriage is a covenant based on love and sacrifice between a man and a woman with vows made publicly and before God—a binding covenant not to be broken. It is intended by God to be a lifelong relationship demonstrating unconditional love, forgiveness, reconciliation, sexual purity and growth.

On the wedding day promises are made out of love for each other and this becomes a legal bond; it is the gateway between the 'leaving' and the 'cleaving' which we read about in the creation story in Genesis 2:24 (KJV) and again in Matthew 19:5 (KJV). Cleaving literally means being glued together; it can be compared with gluing two sheets of paper together and then trying to separate them: the result is a mess!

Adrian and Victoria's story (part 1)

Adrian and Victoria's wedding was one long remembered, not least for the church ceremony itself in Victoria's home village church in the north of England. The church was full to capacity; for those who could not be accommodated the service was relayed outside. Victoria looked stunning in her traditional white wedding dress and was obviously so happy; Victoria's father and bridegroom—both born and bred in Scotland—were resplendent in full Highland dress with their respective clan tartans. The sound of bagpipes greeted them on their arrival at the hotel for the reception and played again when they left for their honeymoon. Nothing was spared for this great day. The previous month Adrian had been inducted as minister of a church 50 miles away where there was high expectation and excitement about the future following the death of their former minister—Adrian looked to be the breath of fresh air the congregation needed. Some from that church had come along for the wedding.

Twelve years later the congregation was stunned when it was announced that Adrian was resigning from his post and rumour had it that the couple were likely to go their separate ways. This news was difficult to grasp for no one seemed to have had any idea that their marriage was under threat. They had started off as such a blissfully happy couple, so totally committed to their calling and to each other.

In those early days Adrian saw himself as being on trial by a congregation who had very high expectations of him in terms of pastoring, preaching and administration. This was a tall order for a young newly wedded man. Within a few weeks of their honeymoon, Victoria in her role as pastor's wife was asked to oversee the Sunday school, the wives' club and the newly established youth club, positions for which she felt inadequately equipped. Adrian had responsibility not only for his own parish but also for two other village parishes; he had no curate and the only assistance he had was from Victoria and from the wife of the headmaster of the primary school, who helped him twelve hours a week with some of his administrative work.

With the arrival of their three children born in close succession it was understandable that Victoria felt she had to withdraw from church activities; the demands of fatherhood forced Adrian into a precarious balancing act in the way he apportioned his time between the family and work. He loved it all; his preaching and pastoring were much valued by the congregation, but he became aware that it was taking its toll. The door to his room in the parish hall was open to all, and the issues with which he was presented made great demands on him emotionally and spiritually. He chose to take Saturday as his day off so that he could spend time with the children, but, like many other young pastors, he had little time for leisure and for being resourced himself.

Sadly, unbeknown to others, all was not well at the vicarage. Victoria was physically exhausted and emotionally drained. Adrian became tired and uncommunicative, and Victoria was resentful of the demands that the church members made on her husband's life and the way in which she was left to cope on her own. She tried to be a supermum, wife and pastor's wife all in one but gradually she saw this as only a pipe dream, and so behind those closed doors the marriage began to crumble. They were both spiritually drained and each felt isolated from the other. Their dream of a blissful marriage and happy family life alongside the fulfilment of a very clear call to ministry was shattered, and the only way out seemed to be to resign and consider separating.

What went wrong? In a nutshell, they tried to do too much. The demands were just too great and sadly their marriage couldn't take the strain.

Causes of marriage issues

Lack of foresight

Many of us enter into marriage far too lightly, not realising that it is a commitment that requires a lot of hard work. We train for many years for our trades and professions and then take refresher courses from time to time while on the job, but, sad to say, those entering into a marriage may see no need, for instance, to attend a marriage preparation course which is available for them. Adrian and Victoria assumed that a few sessions with the minister who was marrying them—a family friend—would be sufficient. Details about the actual wedding service took precedence and there was very little encouragement to talk about other matters. They were ill-prepared for the practical hurdles that lay ahead and, with the birth of their first child less than a year after they were married, they had little time and opportunity to build a strong foundation for their marriage. This foundation isn't built automatically—it needs constantly to be worked at, not least in the early years of a marriage.

Then it is important to remember that a marriage needs constant attention. Just as a car needs regular servicing to function satisfactorily, so does a marriage; if neglected it is vulnerable to breakdown and when the breakdown services are called the repair work is likely to be intensive and painful.

Expectations

A couple enter into marriage with high expectations. They are romantically in love and probably unprepared for the challenges that lie ahead. Preparation courses can highlight the particular issues that need addressing, but good close relationships are only achieved by couples who put time and effort into communicating and nurturing each other. We may laugh about the trivial sources of irritation, such as leaving the top of the toothpaste off or failing to put the toilet seat down, but there can be more serious problems to consider and resolve, such as differing moral values and priorities. Some marriages may run into difficulties because of poor parental role models. If homes have been loveless, with an atmosphere of conflict and abuse, children will grow up with distorted models of married life.

Personal baggage

Alcohol abuse, irresponsibility with money or any one of the other issues tackled in this book may form part of a person's unhelpful baggage. Someone who tends to spend impulsively and makes unwise decisions regarding finance and consequently runs into debt, or is addicted to alcohol, brings potentially destructive baggage into the marriage; much of this may have been unwisely hidden until after the wedding day. Unless such issues are resolved the marriage is unlikely to flourish.

Parents and parents-in-law

Jokes about parents-in-law are classic but not without reason, for if these relationships are poor, they can interfere and create friction between the couple. I know of a husband whose mother-in-law asked for a key to the couple's flat so that she could keep an eye on it; when they returned from work not only had their home been cleaned and the washing up done but their possessions had been tidied away; even the vegetables had been prepared for their evening meal. Kind as this behaviour might have seemed, the wife was not pleased. The mother-in-law subsequently dropped in one evening, letting herself in without so much as a ring on the doorbell!

When I was assisting with a session on marriage enrichment in a church in Hong Kong, I was made aware of the differences between British and Chinese matriarchal customs and how the related issues could create unforeseen problems. Now that churches in the UK are becoming more multi-cultural, cultural differences need to be explored and addressed when a couple are preparing for marriage.

Strangers to each other

Generally the pressures of life are far greater today than they were in New Testament times and neither Adrian nor Victoria had much idea of what lay ahead beyond the wedding day. They had only met a year previously and in some ways were like strangers. They needed space and time to get to know each other in order to build a strong foundation for their marriage but after the wedding they had very little quality time together. Instead of being able to start work on the challenges of marriage, they had to meet the challenges of the church and parenthood. In the early days of their marriage they would start each morning with prayer, a Bible reading and a chat about the day's events. These were precious times, but when Adrian's job became so demanding and his nights seriously disturbed after the birth of their first child, these times were no longer given priority and ended up being crowded out of their lives.

Like many couples, I and my husband were almost strangers when we married, having known each other for less than a year. As we got to know each other better, the 'warts' began to appear and they were not pleasing. With hindsight, it was at that stage that I should have gone for help, but I just let problems escalate and naively thought that, with the passing of time, things would change.

So often when the honeymoon period is over and the flaws in the other person surface, couples become disillusioned and their dream of living 'happily ever after' is shattered. It is in travelling together through the ups and downs of life that love is really tested, gradually changing from a romantic love—one that is steeped in emotions—to a committed love of discipline, trust and sacrifice strong enough to withstand the storms of quarrelling and forgiving, getting real about one another and adjusting expectations. It is when we know we can really trust our partner that we can be totally open and build depth and intimacy into our marriage.

Stress and burnout

Adrian's story is one of stress and burnout. Sadly, this is not uncommon among pastors, especially those working virtually on their own and often responsible for more than one church. In addition to the heavy workload, their hours are anti-social and they are forced to work many evenings as well as on Sundays. This can result in an on-going conflict about priorities and boundaries. It is all too easy for people to put most of their time and much of their energy into church life and have none or little left for home and family.

In my own commuter town I am aware of the enormous pressures on many of the city workers who work long hours with little quality time left for family life. It is no wonder that relationships are put under enormous strain and that marriages may begin to crumble.

Adrian was exhausted emotionally, physically and spiritually. He began to feel abandoned by Victoria in her preoccupation with bringing up the children. They had had such high expectations for their lives together, so that when he realised what was happening to his faith, his calling to ministry and his marriage Adrian felt devastated, alone and helpless. Like the prophet Elijah sitting on his own under the broom tree (1 Kings 19:4), he no longer believed in the goodness of God nor the dictum that 'I can do everything through him who gives me strength' (Philippians 4:13). He had no strength left and, with an intense sense of despair and failure, he seemed unable to trust God's promises. He realised that his endeavours to meet the needs of the church over the past twelve years had been at the expense of his marriage.

Adrian's story is typical of many whose lives are so centred on work and burdened by its pressures that meaningful relationships are neglected. Clearly, heavy workloads and lack of balance in life lead to disaster in marriage, as in other areas.

Children

Adrian and Victoria had little time to build any real foundation for their marriage before the children came along and they became overwhelmed by the pressures of parenthood. The arrival of a first baby can be exciting and positive, but when the second and third come along within a year or two of each other, demands can be enormous. In Adrian's case his time with them was limited due to the pressures of his work. Both Victoria's attention and her affection were now directed towards the children and there was little left for Adrian. He began to feel excluded from the family unit and unable to play his role effectively as a husband or father. I wonder in their case whether the prospect and the reality of having children was ever discussed, let alone planned.

Past sexual experience

A previous sexual relationship, whether or not it has been kept secret, can taint any marriage. It takes courage to share this with our spouse and it may need a suitable Christian leader or counsellor to help. Whatever the area of sexual experience, in order to ensure a strong foundation of trust it is wise to be frank and open with each other and have no hidden secrets, which sooner or later will emerge.

Unfaithfulness

A marriage is built on a foundation of trust and when this trust is broken through an affair, however casual this might be, there can be very damaging consequences. 'Forsaking all others' is part of the marriage vows. What should we do when we find out our spouse is having an affair? Every situation is unique, as is every marriage relationship. If there are genuine feelings of remorse and pleas for forgiveness, there may still be hope for the marriage and it is worth working at. However it cannot be assumed that the marriage resumes as if nothing had happened. Forgiveness has to be offered and received as the couple work together to restore the marriage; they will need not only to forgive but also to free the other person from their guilt and move on. I know of couples who have been able to ride the storm of an affair and experience a deeper and more loving relationship afterwards. Sadly this is not always the case. The marriage may be damaged beyond repair, or the couple may decide to continue to live together under the same roof—perhaps for the sake of appearances or for the sake of the children—but with a relationship deprived of its former love and trust.

Self-centredness

Often the first disagreement within a marriage is when one partner enters into a 'me first' mode. Their former desire to please the other has been replaced by a demand to have their own way. To find that the wonderful person you married has a selfish nature can be devastating. However the realisation that the same is true of us personally is a necessary corrective of our criticism of others. Self-centredness is an issue that all of us need to address if we want a happy and fulfilling marriage. Today, as I write this paragraph on self-centredness, I have just attended a wedding in my church. The address was based on Paul's letter to the Philippians 2:3–5: 'Do nothing out of selfish ambition or vain conceit, but in humility consider others better than yourselves. Each of you should look not only to your own interests, but also to the interests of others. Your attitude should be the same as that of Christ Jesus.' These words relating to humility and selflessness I see as gems of advice for the couple starting out on a new life together, but they can be equally relevant and challenging for any married couple. You may look at your spouse and identify pride and self-centredness, but Jesus says, 'Why do you look at the speck of sawdust in your brother's eye and pay no attention to the plank in your own eye?' (Matthew 7:3). A change in our own attitudes and behaviour, with a desire to nurture our partner, could be a turning point in the marriage relationship.

Re-marrying after divorce

The most common causes of broken marriages and subsequent divorce are unfaithfulness, conflict and incompatibility. Now, with greater cultural acceptance of divorce—including among Christians—many couples find that, rather than working at the issues involved, separation and divorce seem the easier route. Re-marriage can be entered into enthusiastically, but sadly some will just exchange one set of problems for another, such as unhealed wounds, issues concerning the welfare of the children, finance and so on, and the same problems experienced in the first marriage may well re-emerge in the second, not having been adequately addressed.

Priorities

Adrian had a convincing call to the ordained ministry and to a particular church. The expectations of his church were obviously huge and Adrian no doubt had a desire to prove himself in his ministry: to himself, to others and to God. Victoria did not voice her own needs and submitted to what she saw as the more godly needs of the church. Adrian was caught between the two and was probably neither sufficiently experienced nor mature enough to create the healthy balance of priorities required.

Problems arise in a marriage where the spouse is not given first priority. Over-commitment to work or church can override everything else and cause the relationship between husband and wife to fracture. Again, it may well indicate that all is not well in the marriage if more love is given to the children than to the spouse. It is true that love is essential for the security and well-being of a child, but the loving relationship between the child's parents is crucial as well. It takes time to build a strong God-centred marriage, with good priorities, but once established it can, hopefully, ride the storms.

Differences

Apart from the obvious differences arising when one married partner is a believer and the other not, problems can also arise when there are varying degrees of Christian commitment, preferences of church and so on. Tension may also develop when personal views differ on such issues as abortion, ethics, career versus family life and finances.

Marriage brings together two personalities. Some are attracted to a person with a similar personality; others may be attracted to someone with a very different one, who makes up for what the other lacks. For instance one partner may be an extravert enjoying a lively social life and energised by interaction with others; much of their thinking will be done aloud. The other may be an introvert and be energised by periods of reflection; they are likely to be quieter and tend to sort out their thoughts before they speak. Neither is right or wrong, but unless the other person's personality is recognised, accepted and appreciated it can become a source of conflict.

Poor communication

Communication is to do with talking, listening, understanding and empathising. It is not uncommon for a couple to drift apart and stop the sharing of confidences that was their practice in the early days of their relationship. Finding someone to help with their marriage issues wasn't easy for Adrian and Victoria. Their parents were not living close by and they realised it was unwise to find confidants within the church. Having no one with whom they could share, they gradually drifted apart with their problems unresolved and left to fester below the surface. Each was afraid of conflict and wanted to avoid arguments at all costs.

Effects of marriage problems

As we have seen, any one of the causes of conflict mentioned in this chapter can have a serious effect on the marriage. For example, the sexual relationship, which in itself can cause problems, can also be seriously damaged by disagreements, which can affect the free giving and receiving of physical intimacy. Other effects are wide-ranging and vary in their impact.

Lack of emotional affection

The emotional bond that previously helped to keep the couple together begins to wane as the marriage crumbles. For example, the husband starts watching sport for hours and goes to bed late, so that the special times at night when he and his wife used to chat and cuddle disappear. With love having grown cold, conversation is reduced to the mundane and the essential and is often conducted in a casual and offhand manner.

Conflict

Cold and loveless communication may, however, be preferable to arguments, back-biting and having a go at each other; this should particularly be borne in mind when there are children in the home who are likely to be affected by it. Healthy disagreements are one thing, but arguments which become part and parcel of everyday life are another.

Rejection

Rejection by our spouse is a tough experience. We all need to be loved, accepted and affirmed in order to function effectively, so a marriage is likely to be strong when this happens on a mutual basis. However, if things go wrong and the husband or wife starts to withdraw from the relationship, the feeling of rejection can be crippling. This rejection may start to be noticeable when children, church or other things become too important: a husband, for instance, starts to show greater interest in work, friends or sports than he does in his wife.

Moving out

The fear of our spouse leaving us can be excruciating, especially when there is suspicion of an affair. However, when differences cannot be resolved, this may seem to be the only course of action. A couple may well try, over a long period of time, to hide their situation, hoping that the relationship will be restored. A Christian spouse may well have a greater reluctance to break the marriage bond by moving out, with the stigma that can be involved. Moving out may be just one step away from permanent separation and divorce.

Staying together with the problems

Irrespective of the nature of the problems, some couples may decide to put a good face on it and plod on together. In some cases this may involve living under the same roof, reluctantly sharing the same bed, but in effect living separate lives. When invited out as a couple, they will try to give the impression that all is well and may talk to one another in a way that they have ceased to do at home. Even if others have concerns about the marriage, it is hard to intervene unless invited to do so. As for the couple who cannot face up to the pain of exposure and with the welfare of their children at stake, they may try to kid themselves that their marriage vows are intact. To the outside world, everything may seem fine.

Separation or divorce

It takes two to make a marriage but only one to tear it apart. Before God, vows have been publicly made to remain together 'until death do us part'. Christians certainly need to seek wise counsel before breaking those vows, but the chances of saving a marriage when only one partner wants to do so are relatively slim.

To decide to go for separation or divorce is tragic and a hard route for Christians to take. Marriage vows are broken, the couple may face being stigmatised within the church, and then the effects on the children, the wider family and friends have to be faced, quite apart from the financial complexities and implications of the situation.

How the church can help

Leaders and congregation

We live in a society in which biblical values regarding sex and the meaning of marriage are disintegrating. There is therefore a responsibility for church leaders to teach and uphold God's standards by life and by lip. However it is not just up to our leaders to help people develop strong marriages. Within the wedding service at our church we are asked whether we, the family of God, will love and support the couple. There should be a resounding response: 'With the help of God we will!' I am always touched by these words, but also aware that we need to work out ways of implementing them. One way in which we can do so is to encourage all couples to make marriage a high priority in their lives and to keep an eye on those who are involved in Christian service and ensure that this is not at the expense of spouse or family life.

Marriage preparation

Most churches now are able to offer marriage preparation to engaged couples. I have already mentioned the importance of building a strong foundation to enable a marriage to flourish; this takes both time and commitment. If a couple have the opportunity to work through their differences and particular issues before they marry, they are better equipped to deal with the pressures and problems they will inevitably encounter in the future. Such preparation can make all the difference, and it is the responsibility of the church to make it available and encourage all couples who are married in or from their church to prioritise it.

Also, it can be a wise policy to suggest to a newly-wed couple that they have a year out from church commitments, service and leadership roles. During this vital first year they can get to know each other better and actively engage in working at their marriage and building the all-important strong foundations for it.

Marriage enrichment courses

There are now good marriage enrichment courses available which are founded on Christian principles and cover a wide range of issues. Among these is one that now has international acclaim, offered by Holy Trinity Brompton in London and devised 'to help create good foundations for a long and lasting marriage' (see Resources, p. 176). The sessions are designed for any married couple and couple privacy is respected as there is no group discussion and no requirement to disclose anything about their relationship to anyone else. While based on Christian principles, the course is very helpful for any couple with or without a Christian faith. For some it can be a real turning point in a struggling marriage relationship.

Home groups

It could be in the setting of a home group that good role models for marriage can be established. All married couples need to be encouraged to take regular time out together; members offering to look after any children involved may help to make this more feasible.

Adrian and Victoria's story (part 2)

One Sunday just after Easter Adrian climbed into the pulpit and announced his resignation 'for personal reasons'. He mentioned the stress that his work was causing for himself and his family and said that he saw his resignation as the only wise way forward. The congregation were numbed and shocked. They had always seen Adrian as so capable: a good preacher and administrator as well as a loving pastor who met the needs of others in an amazing way. They had no idea of the pressure he was under and of how his dedicated ministry had cost him so much that his marriage was now in tatters. They wanted to lay the blame for what had happened at another's door, and they chose to focus on the senior leadership who were responsible for Adrian's welfare.

Following Adrian's announcement the family slipped away—Adrian to a retreat centre and Victoria and the children to her parents. They needed time to reflect and to restore some kind of equilibrium in their lives. Their friends and families longed for husband and wife to be reconciled and after a few months they agreed to go for professional counselling together. It was hard work but the marriage was saved and a year later, when Adrian was appointed to become part of a ministry team in a city, they moved back together again. They were confident that this new appointment would allow them adequate time and space for family life. This was a happy ending emerging from a sad scenario.

There are actually many stories of reconciliation like this one. The simple message is that there is help available for any married couple and the church should give every encouragement to those whom they know to be struggling, to help them be brave enough to remove the mask of 'We're fine!' and get help.

The power of prayer must not be forgotten and as churches we should be praying regularly for the protection and preservation of marriage.

How people can help themselves

Open up the possibility of dialogue: take the initiative

When we are feeling rejected by our spouse, we can try to communicate our feelings, say sorry for any wrongdoing on our part and assure them that we long to work out ways to restore the relationship. If we can say all this in a loving manner without making threats or raising our voice, it could be very effective. We will have communicated our love and our commitment to the relationship. In a marriage relationship we have the responsibility as well as the privilege of being the primary human vessel of God's love to our spouse, helping them to feel significant and loved. Many a wedding service includes Paul's description of love which is the very opposite of self-centredness: 'Love is patient, love is kind. It does not envy, it does not boast, it is not proud. It is not rude, it is not self-seeking, it is not easily angered, it keeps no record of wrongs' (1 Corinthians 13:4–5). These verses are well worth pondering as we seek to meet not our own needs but those of our spouse.

Nip it in the bud!

There are too many people who soldier on, hoping that things will improve, which is unlikely unless we do something about them. All marriages run into problems that will often have self-interest at the core; when they first occur, the wise approach, as we prayerfully bring the situation to God, is to bring the issue out into the open and tackle it together. Many couples have church-appointed mentors in place from the time of their wedding (these may be those who prepared them for marriage) and if you are unable to resolve your problems as a couple then this would be the time to make contact with your mentors. There should be no shame attached to doing this.

Uncover any hidden problems together

When a marriage runs into difficulties, it may be a symptom of something else going on—an underlying problem known to one partner but not to the other. This could be any one of the issues addressed in this book, such as an addiction—alcohol or pornography, for instance—or a financial concern. Even when these issues have been dealt with, it is wise not to hide what has been going on from our spouse. The freedom and relief that this sharing brings will be well worth it. A depth of trust can be established and there will no longer be that fear of the secret coming to light.

Seek professional help

Bearing in mind the stigma associated with a failing marriage, to admit there is a problem and go for help is not easy; it is wise, however. It takes a brave person to make the first move in a vulnerable situation towards forgiveness and reconciliation, aware of the bitterness, anger and distrust that they might encounter. Even so, it is a step worth taking. But one person's initiative and willingness is not enough. To achieve any realistic measure of success, each partner needs to want to save the marriage and be willing to change. It is never too late to try to mend a marriage, but the earlier we face up to and deal with the issues, the better.

Pray

In any struggling marriage, a crucial step is asking God to show us ways to help restore the bridge between us and to resolve the problems. If another person knows about the situation, we can ask them to pray for us and the marriage. Many people can attest to the fact that God does hear and answer such prayers in various and powerful ways.

How God and the Bible can help

Although there are over 500 references in the Bible to marriage, husband, wife and so on, none directly tell us to how to tackle the problems encountered. We need to rely on the biblical principles given to us, including Genesis 2:24, which tells us that marriage is designed by God: 'For this reason a man will leave his father and mother and be united to his wife, and they will become one flesh'. In marriage we become 'one' physically and emotionally and this should be seen ideally as a permanent bond for our earthly life (but we do not live in an ideal world!).

Marriage can be a beautiful relationship and a mirror of the relationship that exists between Christ and his Church. Paul sees marriage as 'a profound mystery—but I am talking about Christ and the church. However, each one of you also must love his wife as he loves himself, and the wife must respect her husband' (Ephesians 5:32–33).

I believe that for a marriage to flourish, love both for God and for one's husband or wife needs to be central, with attitudes and actions all communicating this. Paul tells the Corinthians that without love he is nothing (1 Corinthians 13:2); and without the foundation of love all relationships, including those within marriage, will fall far short of the ideal and are likely to flounder and fail. However, learning to love takes time and effort. We can draw on God's resources, praying for his help and following the example of Jesus, as well as helping each other and learning from one another the relevant wisdom and skills. Verses 4–13 are worth a place on the fridge or in the bedroom for they spell out the attributes of true relational love on which every marriage needs to be built.

A chapter as short as this can't resolve all the issues that may be affecting a marriage, but it can help to encourage those who say they are 'fine' to be more honest and take appropriate action. This side of heaven, and especially within today's culture, we need to give this potentially beautiful relationship the prominence and importance it deserves.

Prayer for those finding marriage hard going

Thank you, Lord, for the wonderful and amazing gift of marriage. Thank you for giving me someone very special to share my life with. But forgive me, Lord, for often hurting my spouse—my unkind words, the way I withdraw, the things I don't do, my lack of sensitivity, my impatience and anger. Help me daily to put my spouse's needs first, and my own selfish desires last. When I feel hurt, help me to let go of resentment. Enable me to choose to forgive quickly, even when I don't want to. May our love for you and each other grow stronger every day. Amen

Suggestions

- Examine your own life in the light of Galatians 5:22–23 and list the qualities that are most lacking in your life. Ask your spouse or a trusted friend to help you take any action that may be necessary.
- Work out ways in which, as a church, you can help and support marriage. (This could be in the context of a leadership team or home group.)

For those who are married:

- Consider small practical ways in which you can communicate your love to your spouse, remembering that love is not just a feeling and finding ways to make your spouse feel cherished and understood.
- Consider ways in which you can affirm your spouse; this may be through sincere praise, appreciation and encouragement.
- Plan a regular slot of at least two hours each week or fortnight to spend time together. Put the dates in your diary and give these times priority.
- It is never too late to start praying together for a few minutes at the beginning or end of each day. Communicate about the day and pray for each other's needs. Give thanks together for your blessings.

- A strong marriage is built upon trust and openness. Are there any secrets that you know you should share? Consider how you might do this with the minimum of hurt and a willingness to say you are sorry and ask for forgiveness.
- Read 1 Corinthians 13, describing the characteristics of relational love, and apply them to your own life. If you can, discuss these with your spouse.

Chapter 5

Financial issues: getting the right perspective

'Let not... the rich man boast of his riches, but let him who boasts boast about this: that he understands and knows me.'
JEREMIAH 9:23B–24A

He is richest who is content with the least. (Socrates)

Money in itself isn't the problem--all need it to meet individual basic needs. Money isn't the root of evil for it can be used to bring much blessing, but it is the love of it that is the root of all kinds of problems (see 1 Timothy 6:10). Difficulties arise because of our attitudes towards it and our handling of it. A person may be so under its controlling influence that lives can be shattered, as we see in Barry's story.

Barry's story

Barry was an estate agent and when he first started up two or three decades ago, one of his ambitions was to be earning £100,000 a year, which he did within twelve months. The goal soon increased to half a million and on and up until within a few years he had achieved his final goal and had assets of over £2 million. He worked hard and was rarely home before 10 p.m. and then would spend half the night writing up reports ready for the next day. The many hours he previously spent on church-related affairs gradually shrank to very little.

Money and work dominated his life to such an extent that he hardly saw his children and he expected his wife to work in the business—an area totally out of her comfort zone—in order to maximise what he could earn tax-free. Gradually, standards were compromised; also, mistakes were inevitably made because of the ridiculous quantity of work done, and these proved to be very costly.

Following an economic recession and some bad staffing decisions, Barry was made bankrupt. To have to hand over every aspect of his financial affairs to the bankruptcy official for five years was almost unbearable for him. He forbade his wife and children to share with anyone what was going on.

However, Barry and his wife wanted good to come out of this disaster and, for a while, it seemed that it did. They learned to live quite simply. Barry had more time for the family and life was happier—for his wife. Barry started to attend church again—a different one from the one he'd attended previously.

Then, gradually, the compulsion to work and earn took Barry over once again and he was out by 6 a.m. and home late. In the end his wife could stand it no longer and they divorced. However, Barry continued to work as before.

To be fair, Barry was always generous with his money; when things were going well he would buy cars and even properties for friends and families. However, there were strings attached. Barry seemed to think these gifts gave him the right to have some sort of control over the recipients. He was generous to the church, too, and here he gave anonymously. His wife saw this as his kind of penance to God for his compromises in ethical standards.

Causes of financial difficulties

Ambition

Barry's problem was mainly one of ambition; he wanted to prove to himself and others that he could be successful and make money. His ambitious nature could well have stemmed from parental pressure he had experienced as a child. Whatever the underlying cause, he allowed ambition to take control of him and in so doing he eventually sacrificed his relationship with his wife, family and church. He was given a chance to put things right, but after a time he went back to his old ways.

Attitudes

Today's culture, with its love of material possessions, can tempt us into distorted attitudes towards the use of money. These attitudes can change in a radical way when we start to live by the principle that all we have comes from God and we are simply stewards of it. For most of us this involves swimming against the tide of our culture but nevertheless it is a clear witness to our attitude to life itself.

Consumer mindset

I was brought up to buy what I needed: food, clothing, a roof over my head, presents and, when I became a Christian, a 10 per cent tithe to the church. By contrast, in today's culture many overspend and buy commodities that they like, that they can justify but that are not essential. In the present economic climate—and also bearing in mind media reports about obesity—it is sad to see what some supermarket shoppers pile into their trolleys and the amount of non-nutritious foods often included.

Irresponsible spending

Compulsive buying of luxuries is stimulated by the ease of using credit cards and, until the credit crunch of 2008, of obtaining loans and bank overdrafts. There was an era of 'buy now, pay later' and people are still suffering from it as a consequence. It is all too easy to use credit cards irresponsibly, forgetting about the long-term implications. When traders themselves are struggling to make ends meet, we are lured into their shops by eye-catching and appealing special offers tempting us to buy things that we may neither need nor be able to afford.

Circumstances

It is not possible in this short chapter to cover all the eventualities that can contribute to financial struggles. Redundancy is real experience for a few and a threat for many; the wise make contingency plans, budgeting sensibly and cutting out extravagances. However, even with generous redundancy pay-outs, when the household bread-winner loses their job, great anxiety can arise as to whether there will be enough in the kitty for life to continue as before.

Poor budgeting

Many people land themselves in debt owing to poor budgeting. Without financial planning, it is all too easy for expenditure to exceed earnings and for the financial situation to run out of control. Simply hoping for the best is not enough—we need to balance our earnings and expenditure, and keep impulse buying under control.

Tony and Margaret's story

Tony and Margaret have been married two years. They are both in full-time employment: Margaret is a beautician in a department store and Tony is a youth worker in the church which they both attend and where they first met. Tony sees it as his responsibility to handle the household finances. They rent a modest flat on the outskirts of their town. As a youth worker Tony works most evenings, but three or four times a week he manages to meet Margaret after work for a meal. They love holidays and splashed out on a three-week honeymoon in Barbados, but what Margaret didn't know was that Tony had to take out a loan to pay for it. From time to time they go on 'special offer' short breaks to France and Belgium on Eurostar. However, although the basic travel and hotels are bargains, the extras for meals, drinks and treats stretch their finances more than Margaret realises. Unbeknown to her, they begin to fall into the credit card trap and Tony doesn't know how to crawl out of it. With debts piling up he begins to pay one credit card off against another. He is sick with worry, but still he doesn't share the situation with anyone, let alone Margaret. Matters get worse and he even begins to buy lottery tickets, such is his desperation, but the net result is that he sinks more and more into debt. He doesn't know which way to turn. His job as well as his marriage could be seriously in jeopardy if his circumstances were to be exposed.

All this could easily have been prevented if Tony and Margaret had talked openly about their financial resources, agreed a budget and worked within it together, sharing the responsibilities for managing their finances.

Anything is better than the tragic kind of situation where people cannot see a way out of their debts and decide to take their own lives. Such events should be a warning to all of us, within our own families and the church, to be alert to people struggling with such concerns and perhaps too proud or afraid to ask for help.

Love of money

Jesus tells us, 'You cannot serve both God and Money' (Matthew 6:24b). It is so easy to get caught up with this world and its material possessions without fully realising it or reflecting on where our priorities lie. Later in this chapter we will be looking at ways in which we can bring our thoughts and hearts into line with what God desires for us.

Effects of financial difficulties

The effects of wrong attitudes and practices in our handling of our finances, as well as circumstances such as unemployment or redundancy, can be very wide-ranging, as we saw in Barry's story.

Spiritual life

When Barry's ambitions took control of him, he began to withdraw from church life, his relationship with God went into decline and he had difficulty praying. At the very time when God needed to speak with Barry, he wasn't able or willing to listen to him.

Family life

Relationships within the family can be seriously affected by financial problems with disagreements and arguments arising, for example, over the way in which money is being spent. If the marriage is strong then it may well be able to ride out the storm, but if it isn't, things can deteriorate badly, especially if one or other partner (or both) refuses to face the truth and go for help. It is well known that finances can be a major cause of marriage breakdown. As we saw in the previous chapter, building a strong relationship should begin long before the wedding day, with issues such as attitudes to money explored in depth, perhaps within a marriage preparation course. Differences can then be exposed and addressed at this early stage, so that each knows where the other is coming from when a financial dilemma does arise.

Anxiety

Anxiety over finances, especially when debt is involved, is very common and can aggravate an already dire situation. At the Christian counselling service with which I am associated, anxiety is high on the list of primary presenting problems, often caused by hidden financial worries which can, initially, remain unshared in the counselling room. Unresolved anxieties about money can become so great as to affect sleep patterns, eating habits, digestion and efficiency in the workplace, as well as relationships in the home.

Guilt

Guilt is often particularly high on the agenda for Christians with financial problems. The answer is not to give in to despair, but to know that God is there and has promised to meet our every need. He has instructed us to cast all our burdens on him and a financial burden is no exception. If we need to claim forgiveness for any wrong attitudes, unwise decisions or dishonesty, we can rest on his promise that, 'If we confess our sins, he is faithful and just and will forgive us our sins and purify us from all un-righteousness' (1 John 1:9).

However, not all Christians admit to feeling guilty, even those who know they have been managing their money badly, living beyond their means and getting into debt. The desire for wealth can be very powerful, as we saw with Barry, blinding us to the harsh reality of our situation. People can blame the economy and circumstances seemingly outside their control instead of being honest with themselves. It is only when we accept that we are accountable to God for how we manage what we have been given that things can change for the better. With a changed attitude and a willingness to be open about the situation and work on our financial problems, relief and freedom from worry and debt can begin to be a possibility.

How the church can help

Listening non-judgmentally

If we are trying to help others through listening to their problems, a basic principle is to accept them as they are. 'Do not judge, or you too will be judged,' Jesus says (Matthew 7:1). So when someone tells us, for instance, that they are in debt for several thousand pounds, it is not for us to show that we are shocked or to judge them. Jesus wasn't shocked when the woman caught in adultery was brought to him (John 8:3–11). When the person speaking to us is finding it difficult enough to share about the mess they are in, expressing our shock will only make things harder or even bring the time of sharing to an abrupt end. They will almost certainly realise that, as a Christian, your non-judgmental attitude does not mean you approve of their messy situation. Listening can be powerful and can help someone clarify their thinking and sort out their priorities for action.

If we become aware that someone is struggling with a financial issue and we feel unable to help personally, we can try to put them in touch with a trustworthy person with the necessary expertise to help them sort out the issue.

Being there for them

Giving someone practical support and staying alongside them on their journey back to solvency and a new life can make all the difference. Helping them put a budget in place and accompanying them to the Citizens' Advice Bureau or even through bankruptcy and court procedures can be ways of showing love and help.

Communicating what help is available

For most people, finance is a very personal matter, but churches need to acknowledge that debt is very prevalent and there are likely to be church members who are struggling with their finances, whether or not through any fault of their own, and that they may need our understanding and help. An easy way to acknowledge this is through publicising local support agencies. In my own town, Churches Together has initiated a confidential debt advice service where Christians with a wide range of financial experience and expertise are trained as debt counsellors and offer their services voluntarily to the local community. Also, my own church administers a special fund to support those in financial difficulties. This is managed by a team of four trustees with whom members of the church can consult and to whom they can apply for a gift or a loan. In some cases help with money management and budgeting is offered as well as, or instead of, money. On a national scale, on the secular front, the Citizens' Advice Bureau gives valuable advice to people on how to manage debt and recover financially. It is important to make our congregations aware of the help available, by word of mouth and also by displaying contact websites and telephone numbers on notice boards and in news sheets.

How people can help themselves

Acknowledge the problem

It takes enormous courage to lift the 'I'm fine!' mask and acknowledge that there is a problem, whatever the issue. So many of those suffering financial burdens simply muddle along, trusting that matters will resolve themselves, which in most cases is unlikely. Within a loving Christian community, acceptance and confidential help should be available so that people are encouraged to be open and go for help.

Put sensible measures in place

Once someone acknowledges that they have a problem and need help, the causes must be identified and addressed. For some, a good start might be made by destroying credit cards and using only debit cards. Then there is the matter of budgeting. Most people actually get along fine without a budget, but if we are seriously in debt, a spending plan is an excellent way of controlling our expenditures. When the handling of finances is an issue within a marriage, it could help to work out a budget with a friend or professional.

Examine our priorities

The Bible recognises that money is a necessity for survival but continually warns against the love of it. We are told by the writer to the Hebrews, 'Keep your lives free from the love of money and be content with what you have, because God has said, "Never will I leave you, never will I forsake you"' (Hebrews 13:5). This is a reminder to us all, whether rich or poor, that there is simply no security in money and that our ultimate security is in God. This isn't an easy teaching to believe or act on for anyone—particularly for those whose basic needs are not being met so that they are in debt. Even if we are not in difficulties, though, we may find ourselves wanting more and so we ought to heed what the Bible says.

Financial problems may begin to take root when a couple start a family, with a desire to continue with the same home comforts but with less income to provide for them and all the additional expenses involved with a new baby.

Rob's story

When Rob and Sharon married six years ago they were both teaching in the local comprehensive school where they had first met. Finance was not a problem and they were even able to afford holidays in the Caribbean from time to time. However, it was after they moved from their rented flat to a three-bedroomed house with a hefty mortgage and an 18-month-old baby that they began to be stretched financially. Sharon had planned to return to work after her maternity leave, but owing to the onset of postnatal depression she had to give up the idea. Money was tight—a situation neither of them had experienced before. They hadn't always spent wisely but they had always been able to pay off their credit card accounts each month. Now, however, they were finding it increasingly difficult to make ends meet. They hit upon the false solution of paying the minimum, but this soon got them caught into debt. Their marriage had been strong but was now under pressure, owing to Sharon's depression and Rob's concern about their finances. They began to get irritable with each other and to quarrel, each blaming the other for their situation. Sharon wanted at all costs to hide what was going on. Rob didn't agree, and Sharon was eventually persuaded to allow him to share their problems with the home group which he still attended although she no longer did. The group responded with love and understanding. They agreed to pray on a regular basis for the couple and they also asked for ways in which they could help relieve the pressure on Sharon, such as taking round meals and looking after the baby for a couple of hours from time to time.

A few weeks later Rob was called in to see his headmaster and was offered a post of responsibility as Head of Lower School, which came with a substantial increase in salary. Rob was overjoyed and saw it as an amazing answer to the prayers of his group.

At the same time Rob's mother, who was very aware of Sharon's depression and its effect on the family, suggested a two-week holiday for them and offered to come too and help look after the baby. All these things, along with medication, helped Sharon to feel less stressed and even start on the slow road to recovery.

The couple got together to work out a viable budget. Their home group leader was a wise person, able to handle confidential matters, so they asked for his support and help with this.

This story illustrates how a situation can change for the better. Rob was willing to share his needs with fellow Christians. The home group prayed and helped practically. As a result, they all, I think, learnt to trust God more and were encouraged by answered prayer.

How God and the Bible can help

Meeting the needs of others

There is much that we can learn from Luke's description in Acts of the simple yet radical attitude towards possessions that the early Christian converts developed: 'All the believers were one in heart and mind. No-one claimed that any of his possessions was his own, but they shared everything they had... There were no needy persons among them' (Acts 4:32, 34a). Of course, modern situations are not the same as those in the early church, yet the principle of reaching out with love to meet the needs of others is still an excellent one to live by.

Having the right attitudes

Jesus clearly shows us the attitude that we should have towards money. He states the principle that 'No-one can serve two masters. Either he will hate the one and love the other, or he will be devoted to the one and despise the other. You cannot serve both God and Money' (Matthew 6:24). We also have the challenging story of the rich young man who came to Jesus to ask, 'What good thing must I do to get eternal life?' (Matthew 19:16). Jesus' response was: 'Go, sell your possessions and give to the poor, and you will have treasure in heaven. Then come, follow me' (v. 21). Wealth can be a hindrance to discipleship; love of money can be a big obstacle to following Jesus wholeheartedly. Paul tells Timothy, 'Some people, eager for money, have wandered from the faith and pierced themselves with many griefs' (1 Timothy 6:10b). And Jesus speaks of 'the deceitfulness of wealth' (Matthew 13:22) because he knows that to be surrounded with all the comforts that money can buy—none of which may be wrong in themselves—can create a false sense of security.

Being good stewards

We need frequent reminding that all things come from God and that we are stewards of what God has given us. All that we have has been entrusted to us by God and needs to be used wisely for God's purposes. There is a vivid illustration of this in one of the many beautiful prayers in the Bible, that of David in 1 Chronicles 29:10–19, in which shortly before his death he gives praise and thanks to God for the gifts received for the building of the temple, acknowledging that 'Everything comes from you, and we have given you only what comes from your hand' (v. 14b). I know someone who often says that she would love to be entrusted with more money in order to give it away. Such an attitude would make the world a very different place if we all shared it.

Giving willingly and spending wisely

The Old Testament custom of paying a tithe or a tenth of one's gross income to God suggests that giving should be planned and systematic, rather than what we do with our 'leftovers' after honouring our financial commitments. As indicated in 2 Corinthians 9:7, a willing heart and cheefulness should characterise Christian giving, combined with wise judgment as to how we spend our money.

In Matthew 6 the phrase 'in secret' is used four times in relation to how we give; for instance, 'when you give to the needy, do not let your left hand know what your right hand is doing, so that your giving may be in secret' (Matthew 6:3). Our giving should not be motivated by a desire to impress others but should stem from a heart that longs to give. If we give in secret, God will be the only one who knows the full details of our giving, which is perhaps a good principle by which to live.

Whatever our situation, we all have to handle money and the Christian needs to do so with integrity and wisdom. Paul gives wise counsel to Timothy: 'Command those who are rich in this present world not to be arrogant nor to put their hope in wealth, which is so uncertain, but to put their hope in God, who richly provides us with everything for our enjoyment' (1 Timothy 6:17).

Prayer for those facing financial struggles

Dear loving heavenly Father, I want to put my trust in you to help me through this difficult situation. Forgive me for where I have gone wrong and have not been a wise steward of what you have given me. Help me each day to exercise constraint in my spending and to budget methodically what I have. May I never be too proud to accept the help that is available. Thank you that all good things come from you; may I never covet others' possessions but instead be mindful of the needs of others who are less fortunate than I am and play my part in meeting those needs. Amen

Suggestions

- If you are not suffering financial difficulty, in private examine your bank statement and jot down any unnecessary extravagances. Prayerfully decide any action you need to take. What percentage of your outgoings is for charitable giving?
- If you are not living within your means and want to change things for the better, decide on the most appropriate ways forward:
  - Consult with a Christian debt service if there is one in your area.
  - Consult with your local Citizens Advice Bureau.
  - Share with a wise and trusted friend.
  - Ask for help from your home group or church leader or pastor.
  - Pray with a Christian friend and work out your options.
- Work out a spending plan—perhaps with help from someone you trust—that will enable you to manage and control your money more effectively.

- Consider cutting up your credit cards and using only a debit card or neither. Find a suitable budget planner; complete it and keep to it on a regular basis.(see Resources, p. 176).
- Identify—with professional help if necessary—any particular stumbling block or underlying issue that needs to be dealt with which might be hindering you from sorting out your financial problems.
- Read Proverbs 19:17 and 30:7–9. Consider the advantages and disadvantages of being poor and being rich. This might be a good topic for a group study and discussion.
- In the light of Jesus' teaching in the parable of the talents (Matthew 25:14–30), consider the resources God has entrusted to you. How do you plan to use these in the coming years?
- Bring to God any situation(s) where you have not been a wise steward of your money and ask for forgiveness and help for the future.

Chapter 6

Parental pain: tough love

Children are a heritage from the Lord.
PSALM 127:3 (TNIV)

The joys of parents are secret, and so are their griefs and fears. (Francis Bacon)

Parenting is tough and to love our children unconditionally can be tough. This chapter identifies some of the pains of parenthood and addresses ways in which these can be eased. No two people's reactions to similar situations are likely to be the same; upbringing, life experience, personality, age and gender will all make a difference. This is poignantly illustrated in the first story in the next chapter, 'Life after Loss', where members of the same family react to an event in very different ways. Some people are able to share their feelings easily but others, for whatever reason, find this more difficult; in either case there may well be much lying below the surface of which even close friends are unaware.

Books and courses on parenting abound; helpful as these may be in times of difficulty, they are no substitute for having friends, family or professionals alongside who can help make sense of what is going on. Although my experience both in the classroom and as head of pastoral care within a school brought me into close touch with parents, including those who were struggling with particularly difficult issues, this is no substitute for on-the-job experience as a parent. This is why I have included more stories in this chapter. (Caroline is the only contributor to this book who asked to be identified.)

Causes of parental pain
Stillbirths and infant deaths

Caroline's story (part 1)

Approaching the 14th anniversary of Celia's death, it is still hard to commit to writing the chapter of our lives that, to date, has been perhaps the most painful and powerful. It began in a darkened room, full of hope and anticipation, watching an ultrasound scanner's screen —my 20-week scan. Having had a miscarriage earlier the same year, we hadn't mentioned the pregnancy to anyone but had planned to tell family and friends once we had seen our baby for ourselves. Then came the words, 'There's something wrong with your baby's legs.' The ultrasonographer's strained look and difficulty in maintaining eye contact spoke clearly. We were ushered into a pink windowless room with a small table on which lay a leaflet about Support after Termination for Foetal Abnormality. A kind obstetric consultant came in. He told us that, although it wasn't clear exactly what was wrong with our baby, this condition was severe and most probably fatal. My child, whom I had dreamed would play the cello one day, would not live, perhaps not even until birth.

The following weeks were filled with emotional turmoil. We struggled to find as much information as we could about the likely problem affecting our baby. We phoned our local vicar, a number of charities, a neonatal paediatrician, a psychiatrist at the hospital at which I had worked, my godmother, herself a geneticist, and other families who had experienced the death of their first baby. We broke the bitter news to our families—a grandchild, who might not live. We visited a local school for profoundly disabled children—a most moving morning and one which would influence our paths in later years. We went into overdrive to find out as much as we could about the condition and its impact both on the child and on our own emotional, physical and spiritual health, in order to make an informed decision about whether or not to continue with the pregnancy. We wanted to please God in our actions but did not underestimate the physical and emotional strain that would accompany the remaining weeks and months of the pregnancy, our baby's life and early death.

We decided, after much thought, discussion and prayer, including with a Christian couple whose baby son had recently died, to continue with the pregnancy. As my godmother pointed out at the time, that decision was just the first of many tough ones that we would need to make in the journey through our daughter's short life. The remaining weeks of the pregnancy were hard. Nurturing a lively kicking baby whose future in the outside world was so uncertain, with an 80 per cent chance of stillbirth, whose on-going existence we had to justify to some and explain to others, was a lonely experience. I didn't feel able or inclined to go to antenatal classes. We didn't dare shop for a cot or pushchair that our child might never fill.

I can say, though, that in the midst of the great stress and isolation of our choice--regarded as odd by some and cruel by others—we were held and supported by loving family and above all by God, through prayers of so many Christians all around the country and even the world, some of whom we knew and some whom we would never meet and thank. We were provided for in very practical ways by loving gestures such as a place to stay close to the hospital just before the birth. Celia, our first, precious child, was born alive on 16 January 1998, by emergency Caesarean section. We were able to get to know her, to adore her smiles and sense of humour, through the months of anguish and trauma in hospital. We were able to hold her, even to the moment she died, on 5 August 1998, in the peace and quiet of our own home. We continued to be provided for in very practical ways; friends from church cooked meals, others took clothes home and brought them back to the hospital washed and ironed. We were blessed with a place to stay and through visits and long hours of chatting. We knew of much love, of church, family and friends, many of whom met Celia. She had a complete life and left ours scarred but enriched.

The painful experiences of infant deaths and stillbirths—each one so unique in circumstance, reaction and emotion—can last for a very long time and no one must underestimate the depth of the pain. Some couples in these situations may feel particularly uncomfortable to talk about what has happened and prefer emotions to remain private.

As we read Caroline's moving story, no words can convey the depth of her pain in the loss of her young daughter, but in the midst of her pain we have just a glimpse of joy as she and her husband were able to hold Celia in their arms and delight in her smiles. We can also see that the parents were blessed through the loving support of family, friends and church.

Miscarriages

The experience of a miscarriage can be devastating. Statistics tell us that one in five mothers have miscarriages, indicating that many of us have stories to relate of this shattering experience where joy, expectations and hope are turned into sadness and even despair. For couples who end up childless, repeated miscarriages can be deeply traumatic. Here again, those who want to help have to understand that parents may be uncomfortable about sharing the pain of what has happened. On the other hand, talking to just one person or a couple who have had a similar experience may make all the difference.

Sharing our young children's pain

As our children suffer, so we suffer with them; to see one's own child struggling with emotional or physical pain can sometimes seem too hard to bear. This can be the case when, for instance, a child is severely ill or has a disability involving painful treatments. Handing a child over to a nurse in hospital and watching as they are wheeled into the operating theatre can be traumatic. On a different level, parents can agonise when leaving an unhappy child on their first day at playgroup or school. There are a multitude of situations—mostly outside the parents' control—where they have to stand on the sidelines and watch helplessly.

Sam's story

When Sam was aged nine his father's promotion meant the family had to move to a different part of England. Initially Sam didn't appear to have any serious problems about the move and quietly went along with the excitement of it all. However, he later admitted that he would cry himself to sleep at night but didn't share his feelings with his parents as they were so busy with the move and he feared upsetting them. It was a few weeks after the move that he began to show some reluctance about going to his new school. When his father did some gentle probing to find out what was troubling him, all Sam's feelings came tumbling out and they realised how hard the move had been for him; they were devastated at their own insensitivity and felt guilty about the pain that they had unknowingly inflicted on him. For them the move was back into familiar territory, but for Sam it was an enormous bereavement of almost all he had ever known and loved—friends, school, the home and environment where he had been brought up and so on. Everything that now surrounded him was strange and 'foreign'. At his new school he became aware that he spoke differently from the other children, and he began to experience some bullying from his classmates.

We sometimes forget that young children will not have learned the coping strategies that life can teach and may find change particularly difficult in the earlier years of childhood.

During the period leading up to the actual move, Sam's parents were obviously stressed. In their effort not to upset Sam, they tried to help him keep to a normal daily routine. What they omitted to do, however, was to share with Sam what was going on and prepare him for the changes. Children are people with feelings, needs and insecurities and need to be treated with empathy, sensitivity and understanding. A Bible story and a prayer in bed at the close of each day can be an opportunity for children to share their concerns and fears. Sam's parents had huge regrets for the pain they had caused him through their lack of foresight.

Teenage issues

It can be many years into parenthood that the stark reality can dawn—that children are for life! Alongside the joys, we can experience deep sorrows and pain; as they grow older and perhaps life does not work out as they or we would wish, we need to be there for them in those hard times with unchanging unconditional love knowing that at times this love may be openly spurned and they may wish us a thousand miles away! However, it is crucial for their well-being that our children know that they are loved in this way

Amanda and Roger's story (part 1)

Amanda and Roger, who works for an oil company, have four children: two boys and two girls. They attend the local Baptist church, where Roger is a lay preacher, and belong to a home group where the members pray regularly for Roger's witness as a Christian at work.

One Sunday, with the exception of their older daughter, Alison, the family had been as usual to the morning service. Alison, who had just celebrated her 17th birthday, preferred to get up late and lounge around on her own at home. Although she had been a bit rebellious since entering her teens, Roger and Amanda no longer put any pressure on her to attend church, trusting that this was just a passing phase.

It was a sunny June day and after lunch Roger and Amanda decided to relax in the garden. They heard the back door bang and their daughter, Alison, appeared and pulled up a chair beside them. Relationships between them had been more strained than usual recently and it was unusual for her to want to talk with them. Roger's immediate reaction was that she was about to ask for money, so he casually suggested that if she had been about to do that, she might like to consider a weekend job. In reply she blurted out, 'No, Dad, it is not about money, although that could be an issue in the circumstances. I need to tell you I am pregnant!'

The shock for Roger and Amanda was enormous. Despite the fact that Alison had been a bit rebellious, the possibility of pregnancy had scarcely crossed their minds. That sort of problem, they naïvely thought, happened in other families but not theirs. They prided themselves on being good

Christian parents who had brought their children up on biblical principles. On hearing Alison's news, all kinds of thoughts flashed through their minds: abortion, the father, the shame, the practical implications. As if reading their thoughts, Alison drew up another chair and asked if she might introduce them to Alistair, who had been standing just behind them, by the back door. Numbly Roger shook his hand. He looked so young and innocent. Silence prevailed until Alison told them that they didn't want an abortion. Although this would have been an easy option, it was something of a relief to learn this.

Roger's shame was all-embracing. He didn't know how he would face members of his church or his colleagues at work. Already in his mind he had written himself off from preaching and church life. Amanda's feelings were different from her husband's. Seeing her daughter's distress that afternoon, her heart went out to her. Here was Alison, yet to emerge from adolescence, having to face up to the challenges and responsibilities of parenthood. She longed to take her in her arms as she had done many times when she was younger and reassure her that it would be all right. But would it?

When the trauma of the day had passed, Amanda lay in bed reflecting on all that had happened. She seemed to be standing in Alison's shoes, visualising herself as a teenager living in a permissive culture where a high percentage of teenagers now were sexually active. In the eyes of the world she had done nothing wrong. In the eyes of God and the church she had.

Amanda wondered whether they would decide to do the honourable thing and marry. However, although she knew that would make life temporarily easier for all of them, she knew in her heart of hearts that there should be no pressure to do so. It was after much heart-searching that the decision was made to put marriage on hold and for Alison and Alistair to live together for the time being and take equal responsibility for bringing up the child. Better this, it was decided, than the trauma of separation and divorce should this occur at a later stage.

Parents' reactions to a variety of 'teenage issues'—drugs, alcohol, sex, deceit, crime and so on—are likely to be similar to those of

Roger and Amanda: disbelief, shock, shame, guilt, anger and disappointment. Shame can often prevent parents from sharing their situation with others. Sadly people tend to be more fearful about what other Christians think than about what God thinks and this can mean that they lose the support and prayers that could be theirs in their times of crisis.

I recently asked a number of older Christian parents what had been the worst parental pain they had personally suffered, and a number of them indicated that it wasn't necessarily the rejection of themselves as parents (although that was very hard); it was rather the rejection of Christianity that hurt them most. They had to watch their children turn their backs on Christianity, often in their teens, and choose lifestyles contrary to their upbringing. They continued to love their children but agonised, for instance, over their choice of marriage partners, or when what they thought was going to be a happy marriage ended in divorce. Some had the pain of watching their children get involved in drugs, crime or alcohol abuse and end up in prison or having a mental breakdown.

Amanda and Roger's story (part 2)

When I met Amanda and Roger three years later, it was apparent that it had been a rough ride for them both since Alison had broken the news of her pregnancy. As they began to peel off the mask that hid their feelings of guilt and shame, they heard God's voice, 'This is the way; walk in it' (Isaiah 30:21). God had indeed gone before them in so many ways and brought rich blessing to all of them as a family. They now had a delightful lively grandson whom they just adored and none of the family could imagine life without him. Tempted as they had been to leave the church, they soldiered on, but they felt obliged to resign from most of their responsibilities and take lower-profile roles. It was only when they shared their situation with one of the elders and told him how guilty and shameful they felt that there was a turning point. It was pointed out to them that their thinking was distorted and it was wrong to take the blame for what had happened. Their responsibility now was to love and support their daughter and to consider being more open with others in the church. The elder encouraged them to test the waters in their home group; as they did so, instead of the criticism and rejection they had feared, they experienced a wonderful reflection of God's love through the acceptance, understanding and support they were given. They realised they were not alone.

Roger eventually shared the situation with his colleagues at work. Here he and Amanda appreciated the prayer support of their home group. One weekend when Roger had been shopping with his heavily pregnant daughter, he happened to meet his boss. They chatted away normally and on parting his boss wished her well for the birth. The following Monday he was teased about being a dark horse. He was expecting snide remarks about the rights and wrongs of a committed Christian's daughter having a child out of wedlock, but there had been nothing of the sort.

As we see in the following story, it's clear that parental pain can continue well beyond the stage when the youngsters leave to start independent lives.

Rebecca's story

Guilt, anger, shame, helplessness were the immediate reactions of Rebecca when her son told her that he was gay. James was home from university for Christmas. He didn't seem to be his usual chatty self during the festivities and that morning had told his father as he left for the office that he was returning to Edinburgh the next day—-a week sooner than planned—saying he had an important dissertation to complete. He hadn't been in touch with his local friends nor had he been to church, which was very much out of keeping with his normal habits. He had been brought up in a loving Christian home and his faith was important to him. During his gap year he worked in a Christian orphanage in Africa and when he returned he asked to be baptised by immersion in his church as a public witness to his faith. God was central in his life.

James went out for a walk with the dog in the afternoon and soon after he returned Rebecca plucked up courage to ask him what was on his mind, not at all expecting to hear him admit that he was gay. The shock was enormous and she was totally at a loss as to how to respond. As the two of them sat there silently staring into space, she naively suggested that perhaps he wasn't really gay, but that it was just a phase in his development. After all, he had gone out with a lovely girl for several months about a year before. Not knowing what to say next, her son quietly slipped out of the room, but as he went she heard a sigh and the words, 'I knew you wouldn't understand.' That was so true: she didn't understand.

Later that evening the reality of the situation began to sink in. James was their only child. Would this mean they wouldn't have grandchildren? The fact that he hadn't been to church or met up with his Christian friends all now fell into place. Had he told his friends and met with disapproval? She wanted to know whether he had a partner but hadn't the courage to ask, for fear of knowing the truth.

Her husband, Bob, bewildered and shocked when Rebecca told him what had happened, took the view that their son would get over it once he had properly reached adulthood. He was 21 at the time.

Rebecca's pain didn't diminish over the following days. If her son really was gay, what had caused it? Was it due to their bringing him up as an only child? She wondered whether it had been a mistake to send him to a boys' boarding school for the last two years of his secondary education—something he hadn't enjoyed. Had something happened during that time?

As Rebecca told me the story five years later, she was still finding the situation confusing and her feelings of helplessness and guilt were still evident. She is sad for James as she feels his life and all her hopes for it are being wasted. She is sad for herself for she feels she has lost her son. They still meet but their conversations are no longer on any meaningful level and she grieves for the faith he has lost; she is conscious of a huge barrier between them. James, now a qualified radiologist, lives away from home and his personal life is a closed book to his parents.

As a Christian, Rebecca sees that a homosexual orientation is not wrong, but the sexual expression of it goes against her own beliefs and her interpretation of biblical principles. She knows that her thinking is not in tune with that of the wider world and that it is also a matter of heated debate within Christian circles. So she prefers to hide all that she is suffering as a parent and protect herself from the further pain that might be hers through the misunderstanding and criticism of others.

If James does not want to discuss the issue, there is very little his parents can do. However, the parents need not suffer alone and feel isolated. To be able to share and be listened to by a trusted friend can help to alleviate pain and distress.

Let me emphasise that I am not commenting on the rights and wrongs of the issues raised in this story. My purpose is to highlight the feelings of those caught up in the situation.

How the church can help

During their daughter's short life, Caroline and her husband were helped by her church in a variety of practical ways, and the quiet support and strength she received in this way must have been a lifeline. But what about the emotional support following Celia's death?

Caroline's story (part 2)

I had rehearsed the words I would say to friends in the days after her death: 'Our daughter has died.' These words were then—and are still now—met with varying levels of awkwardness. I remember one person saying, 'Well, she was going to die.' I stopped myself from replying, 'As will we all, one day.' Since Celia's death we have been blessed with five more children, but I still double-check myself when asked, 'How many children do you have?' Will I reply, 'Six, one of whom has sadly died', knowing that it will probably end the conversation rapidly and induce a feeling of discomfort in the hearer, or should I reply 'Five' and somehow feel disloyal to Celia? It depends on the mood I am in—on how robust I feel that day.

People are generally very well-meaning, but awkwardness with death can generate some difficult responses that can be very hard for a newly grieving parent.

You need much patience to bear the anger of grief. It is not generally considered 'becoming' for a Christian to be bitter and spit words of pain. So there easily can begin a journey of increasing isolation—trying to lead a 'respectable' existence worthy of civilised society and 'Christian witness' while internally bleeding and dying of emptiness. It is easier to push away well-meaning comforters than to risk hurting others or saying things that they cannot tolerate hearing. It takes a great friend to bear with the true heart feelings of the bereaved.

Every church should work at becoming a loving caring fellowship with members sensitive to the needs of others. A small group could well be the environment where parents in pain will feel secure enough to share their problems, knowing that what they share will go no further, and where they can receive genuine understanding, love and support.

We should all realise that as we seek to understand and support the parent in pain, whatever the cause, this is not necessarily best carried out by *doing* something, or making polite conversation or trying to make the person feel comfortable. It is about simply *being there* for them, listening empathetically and enabling them to share the emotional pain as well as what is going on. This is not a time to be embarrassed by tears or anger or shocked by the way the person perceives a situation. Recently a parent shared with me that she and her husband feel ashamed that their lovely teenage daughter has left home and given up her university place to live with her boyfriend; they find it difficult to talk about it with other parents, especially those who talk about their children being 'believers' and not the least bit wayward. With their love for their child sorely tested, what troubled parents need is a listening ear rather than a critical response.

The church family has a responsibility to every one of its members to welcome them on Sundays and on other occasions with a smile and a gentle word of encouragement. What a difference this can make, especially to those whose hearts are aching. The Christian life is all about relationships—with God and with the other members of Christ's body. Our task is to represent Jesus to those in need and to share his love.

How parents can help themselves

It is a great privilege for children to be brought up in an environment of genuine love where Christian values are practised and each person is totally accepted for who they are and forgiven for their mistakes. Parents have a huge responsibility to model Christian behaviour in their everyday lives. However, when confronted by children who at any stage in their lives decide to rebel against their upbringing, the pain and the helplessness generated by the situation can be overwhelming, especially if the rebellion involves personally destructive behaviour.

Keep loving

Just as Jesus' love to us, his children, is unconditional, so should our love for our own children reflect that same unconditional love. We may not approve of their lifestyle choices, but irrespective of that we must continue to love them and give them the security that love brings. At a time of crisis we may actually be devoid of any feelings of love for them; a deliberate attitude may be what is required.

Guard the marriage

When problems arise with children who are still at home, it is important for husband and wife to work in harmony with joint rules and policies. For example, it is not helpful when one parent tells their teenager that they must be home at a certain time but the other relaxes the rule; this may well result in a child playing one parent off against the other. Marriages can fall apart when a couple disagree over the discipline of rebellious children.

If our marriages are less harmonious than they were previously owing to parenting pressures, what preventative measures can we take? It is unwise to hide what is going on and try to muddle through, hoping things will resolve themselves. A few helpful suggestions could include:

- Listening sympathetically to the other's viewpoint.
- Communicating well and focusing together on the issue in hand instead of having a go at the other person—not saying, 'You never do anything to help!' but telling the other person how you are feeling about the issue and that you need to talk about it.
- Asking for forgiveness when you have done something inappropriate or wrong and having this request received and accepted graciously and not grudgingly.
- Agreeing always to be loyal to one another—not letting the other down.
- Not allowing one partner to walk away from the situation but both taking equal and shared responsibility.
- In the case of rebellious and unacceptable behaviour, working out rules together that can be laid down clearly.
- Trying to pray together, if possible as a family, but otherwise as a couple, using this time to encourage sharing of issues so that they can be prayed about.
- Having regular quality time together as a couple, however difficult this may be to arrange.

Go for help

Parents are often reluctant to seek help, perhaps because they feel either too proud or too ashamed to expose their problems. Some may feel that with prayer, God and the Bible they can solve their problems, but in reality this is unlikely to be the case. Parents need to appreciate that God has provided a wide range of professionals with the right skills to help them. GPs and church leaders can play a vital role in guiding people to the appropriate places for help. Trusted friends who are good listeners can also play a vital part in the process of grieving and recovery.

Learn to be open

Sharing with others has to start with open sharing between parents or, for those who are bringing up youngsters on their own, with a close family member. Obviously, choosing the right person to share with is essential in these vulnerable situations, but trying to struggle on alone, admitting to no one what is going on, means that we lose out on practical help as well as the benefit of having someone alongside to listen and give a balanced perspective on the situation.

Pray

When our minds are crowded with worries about our children, we need reminding that God is faithful and compassionate and also accessible, longing for us to share with him our concerns and anguish and ask for his help. The answers may not come as we would like and anticipate. He may want to teach us more about himself; he may want to change our attitudes. As we read appropriate passages from the Bible and wait on God, our view of the situation may change, and we may begin to experience a measure of God's peace, reassured by Jesus' own words to his disciples: 'Peace I leave with you; my peace I give you. Do not let your hearts be troubled and do not be afraid' (John 14:27).

How God and the Bible can help

A compassionate God

God isn't indifferent to the pain we are suffering. The writers of the Gospels give us vivid accounts of many suffering people who approached Jesus during his ministry on earth and begged for help and healing. And what did Jesus do? 'When he saw the crowds, he had compassion on them' (Matthew 9:36a). No doubt those who watched him closely were aware of the depth of his own emotions— his face, his tears and his longing to alleviate the pain. We have the same God. As we share our parental pain with him and plead for help, his compassion is as deep and changeless as it was then. He can equip us with the wisdom we need for each situation. As we develop a close and intimate relationship with him, he will meet us, hear us and instruct us in the way he wants us to go. 'If any of you lacks wisdom, he should ask God, who gives generously to all without finding fault, and it will be given to him' (James 1:5).

A God we can trust

'Trust in the Lord with all your heart and lean not on your own understanding; in all your ways acknowledge him, and he will make your paths straight' (Proverbs 3:5–6). Trusting in God is such a logical stance for Christians to take—that's a simple yet profound truth. With his knowledge and power, it seems foolish to depend only on our own limited understanding. He knows of our difficulties and longs for us to share them with him, trusting him for all that lies ahead.

A God who communicates

God wants us to have dialogue with him—to communicate our thoughts and desires to him—and as we pray and open up the Bible he can speak to us through the stories and passages we read. Some find it helpful to write down what they see as applicable to their situation. God speaks to us in a variety of ways: through the empathy and love shown to us by our friends and families and within the body of believers, through the wonders of his creation, and so on. He can only do this when we are willing to remove our 'I'm fine' mask and start along a route of openness and sharing both with God himself and, as appropriate, with others.

John White, in his book *Parents in Pain*, speaks about the 'fellowship of parents in pain'—those who together grasp God's hand for comfort and strength.[5] Let us suffer together—never alone —and know that his transforming healing touch of love is freely available for us all.

Prayer for those facing parenting challenges

Father God, thank you for the gift of children and for the love and compassion you show to me as your child. I confess I have found it hard at times to cope with the responsibility of being a good parent. So much seems to have gone wrong, despite all my efforts to encourage my child to live your way. There are times when my pain as a parent feels unbearable. I pray for the strength to persevere, the wisdom to discern and the love to overcome. In faith I entrust my child to your everlasting care. Amen

Suggestions

- Consider ways of keeping in touch with the children of members of your church, particularly when they go to university or move to another part of the country or abroad, by, for instance, sending a card on the anniversary of their baptism, confirmation, wedding, and so on.
- If you know of a parent in pain, pray for them and their children.
- If you are struggling with a concern about one of your own children, as you pray for them make a point of naming things for which you can be thankful. Also, when talking to that child, praise and affirm whatever you can.
- Write down the main issues of concern that give you pain. Discuss them sensitively with your spouse or a trusted friend and work out ways in which you may be able to improve the situation. Bring all this to God in prayer.
- Listening well to our children and to our spouses is vital. Try to pay more attention to listening to others than speaking, and be interested in their viewpoints, even when you don't agree.
- Find out about the groups and organisations that have been set up to help children with their problems and the support groups for parents of children in trouble or suffering in some way. Be ready to benefit from what they offer to you and your child.
- Whatever your experience of pain, reflect on verses of scripture which you find give you comfort and strength. The Psalms may well be a good starting point.

Chapter 7

Life after loss: living fully again

Jesus wept.

JOHN 11:35

Never attempt to hide grief from yourself.[6]

Any loss can bring grief and no two people react to it in the same way: some may be in denial; many feel that life no longer has any meaning; deep feelings of dejection can set in, with thoughts of suicide. Most people suffering loss are able to work through their pain and to reconstruct their lives in meaningful ways. However without the love, understanding and support of others this process can be unnecessarily prolonged. I see the church as being the means of providing the help needed, enabling those who grieve to live fully again. Sadly this is not always the case, as we will see in our stories.

Diana's story (part 1)

Although I knew Diana had lost her son, Neil, in a car accident a few years earlier, it was only recently that I became aware of the depth of her ongoing pain, which she had been hiding from others. A momentary lapse of driving without due care and attention took his life and shattered his mother's life. She had already suffered the loss of her husband at the age of 40 and was now a widow, but she says the pain of losing a son has been even worse for her.

Neil's wife's life has obviously been shattered as well. They had been a happy young family unit with a little daughter of four and plans to have another child. She says she could never marry again, her love for Neil being so deep and the pain so excruciating.

Then there is Neil's younger brother, shortly to be married; over these four years of loss he has not mentioned Neil's name.

Diana finds the burden of grief for herself and others almost too difficult to bear. She regrets that Neil was cremated and not buried. She would have preferred a quiet dedicated space to which she could retreat to aid her along the path of grieving.

Immediately following the accident, the depth of Diana's yearning to be with her son was so great that she seriously considered taking her own life. Strangely and mercifully, she was prevented from doing so through a vivid dream about Neil. This was a real turning point for her and she subsequently realised how dreadful the aftermath would have been of what she had been planning to do. Outwardly she is coping well and she says she is fine; in less than a year she was back in her job within a caring profession. She has, however, a deep inner sadness that she doesn't envisage will ever go away.

Grief is the response to loss and the process of grieving can often be heart-rending, as we see in the stories in this chapter, with each person's loss and suffering having its own unique characteristics.

Although my focus is on life after loss through the death of a close loved one, there are a multitude of other losses in life, all causing grief varying in its intensity: moving house, losing part of one's body or a bodily function, losing a job, a child leaving home, retirement, miscarriage, abortion, a broken relationship. We will explore some of the common threads of grieving running through some of these different kinds of losses.

Effects of loss

'I'll never get over the loss.'

'I'll never get over it' is often the cry of bereaved ones. 'Life will never be the same!' When Diana told me her story I began to see the enormity of her grief and the deep void in her life. She has a sunny disposition and those she meets in everyday life will say how well she is doing. Only the few close to her will sense the pain of unhealed wounds. Although Diana says she will never get over it, it appears that on the surface she is coming to terms with her loss and able to function effectively in her work.

The phrase 'I will never get over it' is common to many bereaved people and in the early stage of the bereavement some may be at risk of taking their own life. Thus it is important for the bereaved person to be encouraged to come out into the open and ask for help. Mothers are naturally close to their offspring, so Diana felt she was losing part of herself and her identity when her son was killed. She could perhaps identify with David lamenting for his friend Jonathan: 'I grieve for you, Jonathan my brother; you were very dear to me. Your love for me was wonderful, more wonderful than that of women' (2 Samuel 1:26). Although still grieving, following her dream, Diana rests in the confidence that Neil has gone ahead of her and that one day they will be reunited. His death could be seen as an *à bientôt* rather than as a final goodbye. Many, like Diana, are helped through the grieving process by feeling reassured and confident that they will meet their loved one again.

Effects on the family

In Diana's story, Neil's mother, wife and brother each reacted to their loss in their individual way; even his young daughter will one day grieve the parent she may hardly remember.

Those close to the deceased person, immersed in the agony of their own grief, are often oblivious of others' sorrow.

We don't know what lies behind Diana's other son's response to Neil's death and his inability to talk about his brother, but this is not an uncommon phenomenon. The emotional relationship to the person who has died is likely to be a key factor in the level of the grief. Someone who loses a brother or sister may well think, 'That could have been me,' or even 'That should have been me.'

Sometimes full grieving can be postponed for months or even

years. Some people do not allow their emotions to surface and consciously refuse to talk about the death. As I wrote in chapter 2, I would have benefited from sharing my loss with an understanding friend at an early stage—talking about the 'lost' person, recalling the details of the death and expressing my feelings and longings.

Effects on spiritual life

Loss brings pain and as Christians we are encouraged to turn to God and to others in our suffering. Some may feel that God has let them down and be angry over an untimely death or being unsuccessful in a job application or being permanently injured in an accident. Those with a strong, well-rooted faith will ride the storm and find comfort in the resources God has available for them. Some in their pain may turn their backs on him, denying the wealth of what is available, not least the fellowship and company of other Christians, and soldier on alone, thinking and saying that no one will ever understand what they are experiencing. Those alongside these people have a huge responsibility to pray that the Holy Spirit will comfort them and also to be willing to be his agents of comfort and encouragement. As the writer to the Hebrews urges: 'Let us not give up meeting together... let us encourage one another' (Hebrews 10:25).

Judy's story

Judy, now 47 years of age, has attended her village church most of her life; she has been one of its key members, leading the Sunday school and recently serving as a church warden. Several years ago she was diagnosed with multiple sclerosis and now her condition has deteriorated to such an extent that she can no longer work. Elizabeth has been visiting her regularly and building up a bond of friendship with her. Together they decided to embark on an enterprise of reading the Bible in five years. They cheated a bit when they came to chunks of the Old Testament that proved heavy going (they think God understands!). However, they loved reading the moving story of Ruth and Naomi and then followed it with the familiar story of Hannah in 1 Samuel 1. Married to Elkanah, Hannah was childless. She visited the temple year after year to worship and pray. She confessed to Eli, the priest, that she was 'deeply troubled' and that she was there praying out of her 'great anguish and grief' (1 Samuel 1:15–16). As Judy and Elizabeth talked together about the joy that Hannah must have experienced with the birth of Samuel, Judy became strangely quiet. Unlike Elizabeth, who had four children, she had none. Tears began to well up in her eyes and as Elizabeth sensitively enquired as to what was wrong she began haltingly to tell her story.

As a nurse Judy had taken her first job at the age of 18 in a hospital close to her parental home and she became an active member of the local churches' youth group. In the Anglican church she attended she became attracted to the curate, Tom, and a friendship developed between them. They would often go out together on Tom's day off, sometimes trekking in the Derbyshire hills and at other times visiting a museum or art gallery in Sheffield. These were treasured times for them and they started to make plans for the future. Unbeknown to Judy, Tom called one day to see her parents and asked for her hand in marriage; it was devastating for Tom when Judy's father refused to give his consent to their marriage (a legal requirement then for women under 21 years of age), saying that 19 was far too young to marry. They had no alternative but graciously to accept his decision. They still continued to see each other but sadly their relationship had gone too far and two months later she discovered she was pregnant. She tried to hide the fact as long as she could and even considered an illegal abortion but eventually she was forced to admit the situation to both Tom and her parents. With utmost speed it was arranged for her to stay with friends of Tom's parents in Zimbabwe under the guise of work experience and further education. There she gave birth to a gorgeous little boy whom she held in her arms just once before he was whisked away for adoption, never to be seen or known about again. She returned to England shortly afterwards and the whole episode was not discussed, even by her parents. Tom by then had completed his curacy and moved away and out of her life. It was as if the whole situation had never happened; she had carried the burden of this secret for all the years since, feeling too unworthy to consider marriage with anyone else. The only person with whom she had shared her story was a Catholic priest in Zimbabwe.

Having this opportunity to tell her story of grief had an enormously therapeutic emotional impact on Judy. It is such a sad scenario: a multi-faceted bereavement of an unusual nature as well as a hidden burden. She lost the child she had conceived in love; she was rejected by the only man she had ever loved; she was rejected by her parents, on whom she had brought shame and who, although still alive today, have little contact with her and no understanding of her on-going pain. Yet another loss was the prospect of marriage— not an option for her as she still carried a burden of shame and guilt and felt unfit for any meaningful relationship. At 19 her life was left virtually in smithereens by these bereavements. She salvaged something from it all, devoting herself to a nursing career and playing a key role within the church. However, lurking beneath the surface was the on-going thought 'If only they knew!' Now Elizabeth knew, and Judy experienced a real sense of liberation.

It was apparent that, by sharing the whole experience with Elizabeth, an enormous weight had been lifted. Elizabeth herself felt privileged that Judy was able to trust her sufficiently to offload her story.

Although Judy had been able to rebuild her life, the quality of it over the years had been seriously affected. Sadly many people carry burdens of unshared losses to their deathbeds. They find difficulty in sharing, owing to the shame of misdemeanours, the fear of losing face with others and of being judged and rejected. Of course, God knows we have sinned and fallen short of his standards, but we don't want to announce this from the rooftops. It is inherent in most of us that we want to hide our weaknesses and failures. To be accepted by others, we assume we should project an image of being a good and strong Christian. However, despite the fact that we would rather not make ourselves vulnerable, being honest and open is the best way forward.

Although her wrongdoing had haunted her over the years, Judy had repented of it long ago and as a believing Christian she could rest in God's promise that, as John reminds us in one of his letters, if we confess our sins God will forgive us our sins and will purify us from all unrighteousness (1 John 1:9). Judy mentioned to Elizabeth that she saw herself as the prodigal son in Jesus' familiar parable: her true father was her heavenly Father who with outstretched arms had shown his love to her, had forgiven her and was always there for her.

The implications and memories of what had happened might still remain with Judy, but the opportunity to share with Elizabeth would have helped to lessen the sting of guilt and the pain of loss and enabled her to focus her mind and feelings on the positive and the good memories.

Maria's husband's death was sudden and unexpected.

Maria's story

I am looking back over the 17 years since my husband's death. What stands out? The early trauma and anguish of losing a loved one suddenly is by no means forgotten but the acute anguish has been replaced, most of the time, by an underlying sadness with which I live.

Increased anxiety is something else with which I live. I have always been a worrier but now I also live with what I call 'flash forwards'—sudden dreads of what might happen to people I love. Just to give one example: if someone I'm expecting is late, I experience sudden and unpremeditated scenarios involving that person having an accident or experiencing something equally terrible. These are very unpleasant but I have learnt not to dwell on them but to push them to the back of my mind. They happen infrequently now and I just accept that they are a consequence of my temperament and what I went through.

In spite of all that, I have learnt and grown in all sorts of ways that have enriched my life, relationships and work.

What helped me most at first and over the years? Above all, people: family and friends whose love, care and practical help supported me and brought me joy, and still does. Some were within my Christian family and there were others who would not have called themselves Christians but, as far as I am concerned, they also reflected something of God's love to me.

And among people I include myself. My choices and my attitude, resulting partly from realising what my husband would have wanted me to be and do, played a part in how my life after loss became a rich and deep experience, albeit a very poignant one. And if there's one thing above all others that I know at a much deeper level than ever before, it is that love is the most precious thing in the world, even though it makes us vulnerable to intense pain.

What about church services and Bible reading and prayer? They had always been part of my life but initially they did not warm or comfort me. They hardly even reached me in my desolation and pain, with one or two notable exceptions. There were moments when some word from God through the Bible or someone else did bring me comfort and reassurance, but for the most part these were like a rather faint and distant light. They have now come back into my life, but not quite as they were before. I have had to rethink it all. I am finding new ways of reading and understanding scripture and of relating to God—ways that are relevant to what I have been through and processed and, I hope, learnt from.

Are there down times? Of course there are. Do I hide them from others? Sometimes I do and that is right. For example, when married friends speak of going on holiday or to the cinema or even being taken to hospital by their husbands, my loss hits me, but I wouldn't for a moment want my friends to realise this and feel that they mustn't talk freely about these things in front of me. I value my friendship with them far too much to want them to 'edit' what they say; besides, I am at the same time delighted that they still have their loved ones. But other low times I can share with somebody face to face or through my writing. And that's helpful and part of God's provision for me, I believe.

Maria's story of life after loss speaks positively of ways in which she has been able to adjust. She admits to private sadness but at the same time is able to acknowledge that her life has been enriched by her friendships and the love and support she has received through them. In rethinking her faith, she has experienced a freshness in discovering new ways of relating to God.

Joy's faith was her anchor through the terrible experience of her husband's suicide.

Joy's story

'Even though I walk through the valley of the shadow of death, I will fear no evil' (Psalm 23:4). Few words could have been more poignant in the days after my husband's death. For I have walked that walk, with him, through that valley, not only in the days immediately after but even now.

For him it would have been an unbearably agonising walk but a short one. For me it is a daily walk and one I am destined to undertake perhaps for many years to come. Without God's rod and staff (v. 4) it would not be one I could even embark on. As it did for him, it would overcome me.

For it was not like the walk we are all destined to take at the end. He did not want to die; he just wanted the pain to end. And the pain was nothing that the ordinary person could understand; mental pain is so very much worse than even the most severe physical pain. People die of the most severe physical pain and there is only sympathy for their suffering and for those left behind. People die of severe mental pain and there is not sympathy but only questions. Why? And for those left behind there is such a different sort of sympathy, almost distrust, a stigma and, most painfully, an inability to acknowledge the death or allow outward shows of emotion.

As for me, I feel utterly isolated. People don't talk to me about him. For them there is no 'him', only unanswered questions about his death. There is so little interest in how he lived and so much interest in how he died. But his life was no less remarkable than that of someone who died a socially acceptable death. They can be talked about; their life can be acknowledged. But all his achievements, his great qualities and everything he gave to others are forgotten.

Please, God, let him have been killed in war. Let him have died in a road accident. Then I could talk of his death without fear and of his life with pride. People could outwardly acknowledge my suffering and trauma. But as it is I must carry my pain alone, hang my head in shame and quake with fear should someone ask how he died.

Yes, suicide is probably the most difficult sort of death to understand and accept. But in order to begin to understand we must not judge the person who has died; so often they did not die by their own hand but by a modern-day debilitating cancer called depression. Understanding, acknowledgement and acceptance would help me and my children so much more than avoidance and judgment. We loved him no less than a person who was not ill; indeed we loved him deeply and with real intensity. The hole left behind is just as deep and just as gaping however it came about.

Such deep and personal pain from the loss of loved ones forces doors to open into the depth of the soul, causes people to re-examine their faith and relationship with God and others, and can eventually bring them to a new and good place. The pain may be excruciating but lessons can be learnt through it that can be profound and ultimately enriching.

Although suicide has not been a crime for a long time, sadly it still has a stigma attached to it. For the bereaved there is acute sensitivity to the hidden thoughts of others—blaming and judging. Joy longed to be able to grieve like any other widow and to be able to talk about her husband, but she felt this was denied her. She was suffering unspeakable pain but, because his death was socially unacceptable, she felt she had to carry it virtually alone.

My own story

In the chapter on depression I shared something about my own experience of loss. It is now many decades since my bereavement but I still grieve my loss and the life that would have been ours, perhaps with children and even grandchildren. We talked together shortly before his death about my future and the memory of that conversation is still vivid in my mind. More than anything else, he desired my happiness and ideally wanted me to marry. However, when he died, something in me died too. I had to make the choice and try to come to terms with life without him, but, although I did marry later, it did not work out as I would have wished. Most of my close friends have grandchildren with lives revolving around them. I am delighted for the joy they receive through them and, like Maria, I would not have them 'edit' what they say, but nevertheless I do grieve, as it were, for the grandchildren I never had.

However, my life has been shaped by God in ways I would never have envisaged. I have been able to move on from past sadnesses, disappointments and failures with a deeper and closer walk with God. He has allowed me to develop my gifts for his purposes and given me opportunities to use these and my experiences of life to help and encourage others. I have been the recipient of God's amazing grace and many blessings, not least through loving and caring friendships he has provided. Vital to my well-being is to put my trust in God for the choices I make each day, but I still have much to learn in this school of trust.

How the church can help

Diana's story (part 2)

At her times of need, when she lost her husband and again when she lost her son, Diana turned to the church she attended for help and support. In her first bereavement she was invited to a bereavement support group. However, the others within that group were widows much older than herself with whom she felt she had no real affinity. When she lost her son the pastor did visit her—which she valued—but only once. After church services hardly anyone spoke with her, despite the fact that she had been mentioned in the prayers. All this was painful for her. Eventually she gave up attending that church altogether.

This story speaks for itself and has lessons for each of us. Avoidance seems to be a classic British reaction to bereavement and causes untold pain. We don't necessarily need to say much, but just be prepared to listen. If this proves too difficult, the very least that can be done is to send a card, but better still is to extend a simple invitation to the person such as going out for coffee. Even if our invitation is declined, it shows that we care. Our church leaders need to be proactive in setting up support groups or at least being able to point people in the right direction to find one.

Maria speaks about the love of God shown through her friends, which she experienced at a much deeper level than ever before. This resource helped to lessen the pain of her grief, brought her the comfort she craved and enriched her life.

Joy had for many years been close to her church fellowship, yet when she needed them most she felt somewhat ostracised; not only did they having difficulty in knowing what to say, but also they were curious to know the 'whys' and 'hows' of her husband's death. She longed for comfort in her pain, but instead she sensed a judgmental attitude towards what her husband had done—'Fancy inflicting such pain on the family!'—and even towards herself—'Must have been something wrong with the marriage!' Such attitudes, whether expressed or simply sensed, accentuated her pain.

Those who grieve the death of a loved one need both solitude and community to help ease the pain and bring healing and restoration into their lives. Solitude brings comfort from God; community offers God's love through relationships. Grief is not easy for any of us and we may well find that our pain is so overwhelming at first that we are unable to talk about it. However, when we are ready, we should be able to find within our church an established culture of love, acceptance and openness in which the bereaved can talk about death, including suicide, without fear of judgment. The church's function as a body of believers is simply to love, support and listen to the anguish of those whose lives have been torn apart through loss, whatever its cause. We will not always get it right and much sensitivity may be needed in each situation, but may our churches be known as communities of compassion and prayer, ready and able to point those who are suffering to Jesus himself.

How people can help themselves

By our attitudes

Grief is part and parcel of life. Loss often comes without warning, however, and we are unprepared for it. Either it can consume us, sending us down paths of self-pity and withdrawal from others who 'don't understand', or we can come out into the open, and, in our vulnerability, accept the loving care of others. At the end of this chapter there are a number of practical suggestions about ways in which we can help ourselves to ease the pain and move on.

By learning to adjust and accepting help

One of the classic and necessary stages of the grieving process is that of adjusting to a new phase of life and moving on, something that is rarely easy to achieve. It seems safer and less painful to continue hiding from others and remaining inactive. Only last week I met with someone who lost her husband a number of years ago but admits that she hasn't been able to regain any meaningful quality of life without him.

The first step towards helping ourselves may be to find a good listener who will come alongside us and hear our pain. This could be a professional counsellor, a pastor or a good friend—someone with whom we feel totally comfortable, who is willing to hear our story and who can empathise with our feelings and, in due course, once the healing process has begun, stay alongside us and encourage us to move on. After all, our loved one who has died would surely want this for us. For their sake and our own we must not refuse the support of those who will give us the help we need to begin the necessary adjustments in order to 'get a life' rather than simply 'get by'.

How the Bible and God can help

To a person of faith who believes that God can prevent tragedies, it is quite understandable that Diana was angry with God and that her feelings of anger were not helped by the lack of support she received from other Christians. Many years down the line she may be in a position to evaluate God's purposes and assess the ways he has brought blessing and growth from the tragedy—this is a common experience for many Christians, despite their initial anger and grief. In my own loss I was poignantly reminded that in this transient life I was just a traveller in a foreign land with heaven as my ultimate destination. Loss can cause us to question our spiritual values and beliefs, but we can come out on the other side stronger and more dependent on the resources God has in store for us. This is evident in Maria's story.

Joy, whose husband died so tragically, writes that without God's presence 'through the valley of the shadow of death' (Psalm 23:4) she could not have continued on her journey through life. She is bravely walking that walk with God 'by faith, not by sight' (2 Corinthians 5:7). For her it's a blind road ahead but she has as her guide Jesus, in whom she is able to trust as 'the way and the truth and the life' (John 14:6). Although the wounds of loss may be deep, we must trust God in his ability both to heal and to give us hope for the future. When the pain is still with us, the 'I'm fine!' mode is neither wise nor helpful in this healing process. Whether a helper or a sufferer, as believers we are members of the body of Christ, created for relationship with God and others. As such, God commands us to love him and our neighbours. And within this command is the willingness to give and receive a helping hand to those living with loss. We then can move forward together into God's shelter where 'he will cover you with his feathers, and under his wings you will find refuge; his faithfulness will be your shield and rampart' (Psalm 91:4).

Prayer for those enduring grief after loss

Dear Lord, uphold me, I pray. Walk by my side through each day. You alone know the depth of my sadness, the loss I carry in my heart. Console and comfort me, Lord, in my loneliness without [name of loved one]. Help me with my burden of grief; help me under the weight of my sorrow.

Be with me each day as I try to cope, as I strive to lead a normal life, and help me relate to those around me. Be with them, too, as they care for me. Give them the right words to speak to me, words of comfort and words of hope. Let the love of your dear Son, Jesus Christ, shine through them. And, Lord, allow me at the end of my time here on your earth to be reunited again with [name of loved one] and to live with you in the joy and peace of your kingdom. Amen

Suggestions

- You may not be feeling good about life right now, but you can still bring to mind things for which you can be thankful. Jot these down and offer your thanks to God for them.
- Identify a loss in your life. What changes—for better or worse—have you seen in yourself as a result of the loss you have experienced, in terms of attitudes, insights, skills, and so on?
- How has your view of God and your relationship with him been changing since your loss?
- Identify those in your life who have been a help in any grief or difficult circumstance you have experienced. How have they helped?
- Identify ways in which your church could give more support to those who are suffering the pain of loss.
- Identify someone in your church who has suffered a recent bereavement. Write a prayer to God for that person. Think of ways in which you and others can help them and show God's love to them.

Chapter 8

Addictions: released for life

'You shall have no other gods before me.'
EXODUS 20:3

Addictions bring short-term pleasure but long-term pain and limitations.

What do we mean by addiction? An addiction is a physical or mental dependence on a substance or a behaviour which becomes harmful and which the person feels powerless to stop. Alcohol, drugs and pornography are said to be front-runners but there are a host of others—gambling, technology, sex, exercise, food, work, shopping, religion and any number of other practices that either dull pain or excite the mind. As someone develops a dependency, the brain chemistry starts to adapt and then demands more, so that withdrawal has to be medically controlled. Other parts of the body can be affected, such as, in the case of alcohol, the liver and, in the case of tobacco, the lungs and heart.

Some people's addiction takes a religious form: they may seek to avoid pain and overcome shame by adopting a narrow and rigid approach to life by, for example, engaging in obsessive praying, being over-zealous about going to church or reading and quoting scripture non-stop. This approach to religion is really idolatrous and negates the possibility of any genuine personal relationship with God. Addicts see this as a 'good' addiction, since it involves a 'good God', hence they feel no shame about their behaviour as it can be justified through scripture.

Addictions bring short-term pleasure but may cause long-term pain and limitations.

Nick's story (part 1)

I met Nick in France, where we were both employed by the Air Ministry: he as a medical doctor and I as a teacher. He looked after my body, I taught his children in the week and he taught other people's children on Sundays. Many years later, I bumped into him in London. At first I hardly recognised him—he was haggard and bent, very different from the upright and handsome man I had known. He seemed pleased to see me and we agreed to have lunch together the following day.

Nick's story was a sad one. In France he appeared to drink in moderation, in common with his colleagues. He looked and acted as a relatively contented man; he wasn't bleary-eyed, functioned well in his work and was much loved by his patients. No one knew he was actually an alcoholic.

Unbeknown to me at the time, Nick had a very poor relationship with his junior doctor, Bill; they were like chalk and cheese in temperament. Nick was always punctilious in his work, but Bill was laid back and tended to cut corners, so that Nick was often left to pick up the pieces—no easy task when people's health and lives were potentially at risk. Instead of being grateful to Nick for covering up his mistakes, Bill became insulting and aggressive. Most of Bill's patients didn't particularly like him and preferred to be treated by Nick, who had a heavy workload as a result. All this took its toll on Nick. Rightly or wrongly he didn't want to expose Bill's mistakes to his seniors so he battled on, unable to share his concerns with others. During the latter half of his three-year tour of duty he had begun to drink heavily, mostly at home. His children—in their early teens at the time—were unaware of any problem and even his wife had no true picture of the amount of whisky he was consuming on a daily basis.

Nick loved Sundays when he wasn't on duty. He normally attended the American chapel services and when he was asked to take a Sunday school class he readily accepted. He enjoyed serving in this way—it felt like an antidote to his problems that he was doing something for God.

Shortly before he was posted to Germany, he was called for a routine medical examination and his alcohol problem finally came to light; it had taken hold of him and was beginning to destroy his body and his life. So he vowed to limit his drinking to three glasses of whisky a day; he knew that if he didn't he would probably lose his job. But to his dismay he was asked to see a psychiatrist when he moved to Germany.

Up to this time Nick had done well in hiding what he knew now was an addiction. When his wife was asked to accompany him to a psychiatric clinic, she was totally aghast to hear the seriousness of the situation and that his drinking was in fact an addiction.

Together Nick and his wife worked hard at trying to reduce his consumption. All went well for a while but gradually the whole situation spiralled out of control. He quietly left the RAF on medical grounds and agreed to seek help.

What next? His life was in tatters. He owed so much to his wife, who never ceased to love, help and support him, although she was enormously affected by the trauma. She stood by him faithfully until her sad death three years later from a stroke, shortly before I bumped into Nick. He felt massive guilt and was struggling to restore a meaningful relationship with God.

'A waste of a life!' was my immediate thought, but I also felt pity for his brokenness. Why did a normal middle-class professional man—a doctor to boot—not have better control of his life? Where was God in all of this?

What were the effects of Nick's alcoholism? It had a disastrous effect not only on himself but also on the family. He had the privilege of a loving, understanding and supportive wife but who is to say whether or not her stroke was due to the stress of the situation? He lost his job with inevitable financial implications, and his career in medicine was ruined. His deep feelings of guilt about his addiction gradually became incompatible with his faith and he ended up deep in grief for his old life, with all its potential, that he had lost.

Causes of addictions

Insecurity and lack of love

As human beings we all have a deep basic need for love and security; those who have been deprived of this in childhood have increased vulnerability to addictions.

Genetic predisposition

There can be a genetic predisposition to addictions. This means that if someone overcomes one addiction, they are likely to succumb to another. For some this can prove a lifelong battle.

Stress

We often hear of those who 'turn to drink' for relief when life becomes tough and there is no imminent prospect of changed circumstances. Nick's stress, caused by his job and the strained relationship with his junior doctor, contributed to his alcoholism. Alcohol dulled the pain and helped him to cope. Many people now, wanting to relax at the end of a busy day, can be found glass in hand soon after returning home from work. Sadly, this habit can escalate, as it did for Nick, for both men and women.

Feelings of inferiority

Those struggling with feelings of inferiority, low self-worth and shyness, and with a desire to be more socially acceptable, can find that alcohol or drugs can make all the difference, temporarily dulling their anxieties and enabling them to overcome their inhibitions.

Social issues

Many youngsters grappling with situations of unemployment, inadequate housing and strained relationships in the home are left feeling hopeless and purposeless. They can be particularly vulnerable to misuse of alcohol, drugs and gambling to help lift them from their depressed state.

Poor role models

Those brought up in homes with poor role models in terms of addictions, where for instance alcohol or drugs are abused, are clearly at greater risk of becoming addicts themselves.

Loneliness

Loneliness and isolation. with accompanying feelings of depression, anxiety and fearfulness, can make a person susceptible to an addiction. This is not uncommon among older people, who can be very skilled at hiding their harmful habits.

Spiritual void

In far too many homes across society there is an absence of moral and spiritual values, which can give rise to feelings of emptiness and meaninglessness. Without any satisfactory answers to questions such as 'What's it all about?' and 'Why are we here?' life can start to feel pretty pointless. An addiction, although never truly satisfying, can be used to take the place of God and the wholeness in life that he has to offer.

Common addictions

Alcohol

Most people with an alcohol problem are normally in denial to others and even to themselves that they are drinking too much. Initially they assume that they can give up the habit. It can take a catastrophe such as Nick's to admit to what is actually going on, but even then people may refuse help, assuming that it is within their control to do something about it. Alcoholism can creep into lives so easily. Alcohol is freely available and in itself having a drink is not seen as anything wrong. When people are vulnerable to it, for whatever reason, it takes them in an iron grip, damaging both them and others.

Addictions: released for life

Gambling

Jimmy's story

When Jimmy returned home from work one evening he was confronted by a distraught wife. Catherine had just had her debit card refused in a local supermarket and upon investigation with the bank she discovered that their account was overdrawn. She assumed that fraud was involved; not for one moment did she suspect that Jimmy was at fault. He was 'upright and God-fearing', as his parents described him to her when they first met; she depended on him for everything and she felt sure he would be able to sort things out. Money had always been tight, but the situation had grown worse in the past year when Jimmy had been out of work for several months and Catherine had become a 'dinner lady' to earn a bit for the household pot.

Jimmy adored Catherine. They had been married for two years and were anxious to start a family. He wanted to show his love to her and would frequently give her presents and take her out to a local restaurant. What she didn't know was that he couldn't really afford any of these 'extras'. While most people dabble in gambling at some point, if only at the funfair, Jimmy was brought up with a very legalistic Christian mindset; gambling would certainly have been among the 'thou shall not' family commandments. This makes it all the more surprising that Jimmy started to participate in something his parents saw as a 'deadly sin'! Initially he had been looking for a short cut to provide money for extras for Catherine. What began as a small flutter at a high street betting shop became an obsession over which he eventually lost control. He won over £100 that first day, enabling him to take his wife away for a weekend, telling her that he had received a small bonus from work. And so it went on: winning and losing, getting more and more into debt, paying off one credit card against another. Then came the day when Catherine asked what had happened to their household bank account and he had little alternative but to come clean. To his wife, the deception was incomprehensible. Jimmy felt like a criminal; he was riddled with guilt, devastated that gambling had become his master. At other difficult times in his life he

133

had called on God to help him; now he felt he couldn't. He knew his gambling was wrong but couldn't extricate himself from it. As a result he felt completely trapped and totally estranged from God.

Jimmy's deception, lies and obsession with gambling were obviously wrong, but what about gambling itself? There are no direct references to it in the Bible. We read about people 'casting lots' when a decision had to be made—Joshua cast lots in Shiloh 'in the presence of the Lord, and there he distributed the land to the Israelites according to their tribal divisions' (Joshua 18:10). We read in Acts 1:26 of the disciples casting lots to replace Judas who betrayed Jesus. Casting lots—simply the same as throwing dice or flipping a coin today—was a simple way of settling disputes and making impartial decisions, so that no one could argue the decision was the result of politics, nepotism, favouritism and so on.

Many Christians are brought up to see gambling as wrong, because it is based on luck and luck is not part of a Christian's vocabulary. In a number of churches, raffles and bingo are not encouraged. I sometimes wonder what would happen if a church leader won the National Lottery at a time when church funds were at a low ebb!

Those whose gambling has spiralled out of control may manage to hide their addiction as Jimmy did, with cover-ups and untruths about the extent of their debt; some really seem to believe that when they win the jackpot all will be well, and it is tragic to see this deception becoming a way of life for them.

When Jimmy shared his problems with his pastor he was at pains to defend his action, stressing that he was primarily motivated by love for his wife. He liked to receive presents from loved ones himself, so he assumed his wife did as well. As she gradually became a part of the counselling process she tried to help him understand that there were many other ways in which he could communicate his love for her. She didn't need presents.

It was devastating for Jimmy to be forced to expose his deceptions and addiction. However, as he looked back, he saw this exposure as providential. Not everyone will have an understanding wife like Jimmy's, who supported him through the complexities and terrible aftermath of that first innocent flutter. During this whole episode God seemed many miles away, but eventually Jimmy was able to ask for forgiveness, knowing that he was no longer under the control of his gambling. His restored relationship with God was overwhelming and life changing.

Pornography

Pornography is a hidden addiction that can take place without anyone knowing but is devastating when the secret is exposed.

Chris's story

Chris became a believer in Jesus while a member his church youth group and was all set to leave for university when a major upset happened at home. His father had been spending an unusually long time late at night searching the web on his laptop, so much so that Chris's mother wondered what was absorbing so much of his interest. He was not very clever at covering his traces on the internet, and Chris's mother was devastated to discover he had been looking at pornographic pictures.

She was so distraught that she talked about walking out of the home, concerned for the protection of her precious daughter. It was at this point that Chris went to his pastor and asked for help. What was he to do? How should he comfort his sister? Should he talk to his dad? Was there no way to keep the family together? The pastor told Chris that it was unlikely his dad would do more than make excuses if he tried to talk over the issue with him. But he urged Chris that, if a natural opportunity arose, he should encourage his dad to call the pastor to share his side of the story.

Shortly before Chris left for university, his dad did go and see the pastor. He was contrite but reluctant at first to accept that without counselling and prayer he would not be able to conquer his addiction to pornography. For Chris, university was a happy withdrawal from the stress of trying to love his father and mother while not taking sides. He would e-mail his pastor to let him know how things were going with his dad, but it was clear that his mum felt so betrayed that she found it hard to rebuild the trust she had had in her husband.

Chris's mum decided to move out of the home with her daughter, going to live with her sister. His dad was left isolated at home, desperately trying to get his family back together. In the crisis he turned to God for help but his recovery was a long and painful journey. On reflection, he wondered why he had allowed himself to search the internet in the first place. He came to see that his sex life had became routine, and his wife reacted to this with understandable coldness, at which point he gave way to lust and allowed the love between them to wither and die. He had learned a hard lesson.

Men turn to pornography for a variety of reasons. Chris's dad's sex life had lost its love and romance and had become routine. Pornography appealed because it offered physical gratification without having to face all that is involved in the intimacy of a marriage relationship. An image on a computer may stimulate sexually for a while but then a desire develops for more explicit images, which can lead to addictive behaviour that is hard to stop unless the person is determined to do so. Paul gives instructions to the Colossians for holy living: 'Put to death, therefore, whatever belongs to your earthly nature: sexual immorality, impurity, lust, evil desires and greed, which is idolatry' (Colossians 3:5).

Effects of addictions

As we have already seen, most people do not deliberately set out to become addicts. Younger people may just want to experience something new, but whatever the original reason, the behaviour can spiral out of control and cause havoc in its wake.

On the brain

We are aware that even after only a few drinks people may undergo a distinct change of behaviour—slurred speech, difficulty in walking and slow reactions. At the weekends hospital accident and emergency departments are full of the victims of alcohol-related violence and those who have made themselves ill through over-drinking. Clearly any drinking has a direct effect on the brain, but when it is done to excess, as in other addictions, the damage can be severe for it causes changes in brain function that are difficult to reverse.

Loss of sexual libido among young men, when sexual desire should be at its peak, is now common with those who repeatedly view pornography on the internet. This is due to the over-stimulation of dopamine in the brain—the neurotransmitter that activates the body's reaction to sexual pleasure. The same occurs with a shopping addict on a shopping spree when a feeling of euphoria is created. While engaging in these activities, dopamine is triggered and released. The brain cells get accustomed to having that amount of dopamine present and, as the brain gets used to this stimulation, it requires more and more dopamine to achieve the same effect. When the dopamine-producing behaviour is finally stopped, the brain has to get used to lowered dopamine levels; this can cause cravings and withdrawal symptoms.

Physical

Addictions affect people physically in different ways depending on the person and the circumstances. The following physical effects may occur:

- cancers
- heart disease
- heart attacks and cardiac arrest
- cirrhosis of the liver
- weight problems
- sexual problems: lack of sexual desire—particularly through exposure to pornography
- depression—particularly through alcohol abuse.

Family life

Addictions not only affect the person but also often create family problems, as the stories in this chapter have shown. Marriage relationships can be put under enormous strain due to:

- deceit/suspicion
- financial issues
- criminal issues
- inappropriate/anti-social behaviour
- sexual problems
- physical problems
- detachment from family/changed priorities.

Any one of these can aggravate an already existing tendency towards a particular relationship issue.

How the church can help

Put yourself in the shoes of someone who is a member of your church hiding his addiction to porn yet desperate to rid himself of it. Where would you turn?

Professional helplines

Website and phone numbers should be clearly displayed within the church building and perhaps even outside on church notice boards. In our church we have bookmarks listing helplines which have been distributed to each member of our congregations and are now available on our welcome desk.

Pastoring

As we have seen, those with addictions can have enormous difficulty in admitting their problems. So within a church setting it should be made as clear as possible whom people can turn to within the church for confidential pastoral help.

Friendship
The addict will need massive love, understanding and support as they break their habit and start on the road to recovery and towards fullness and wholeness of life.

Professional help
If someone were to come to me asking for help with an addiction, I would encourage them to make contact first with their GP. If they are reluctant to do this, I would direct them to a local counselling service or to a specialised group such as Alcoholics Anonymous. I would also suggest that at the same time they look for spiritual help from their church pastor or elder and that they be more open about their situation, as both Chris and his father were. By this I don't mean to put it in the weekly news sheet! To admit to being addicted to porn, for instance, requires enormous courage, so once someone admits to needing help, access to professional support must be made as easy as possible. And we shouldn't forget the addict's family—the spouse in particular—who may also need help and support.

Teaching
Any addiction will have a serious effect on both family life and the individual's relationship with God. I am aware that the use of pornography is widespread within the church but sadly this addiction is likely to go unchecked for it comes with so much guilt and shame, unacceptability and taboo. As a result, it is kept hidden, but even so it destroys relationships, as we saw in Chris's family.

The church's role is to teach the beauty of relationships, that the marriage relationship can be the richest relationship of all and that addiction to sex, apart from that loving committed relationship, debases our humanity and makes us slaves to self-gratification.

The church should teach about the dangers of all addictions, because of the way these can take control of lives, drawing the victims away from God.

We have all sinned and fallen short of what God requires of us, so we shouldn't judge others but rather focus on ways in which we can love, support and care for people in their failure and weakness.

Nick's story (part 2)

Nick's drink problems had created a barrier between him and God. As he described it to me, he felt spiritually dry yet thirsty for the relationship he once had. On returning to the UK, he and his wife had moved to a village where they cautiously started attending a local church where they felt at home. It was here that Nick was able to begin his journey back to intimacy with God. His mask had been removed and the face he showed to the outside world was a genuine and honest one. He was open about his addiction and past life and within this church he found understanding and acceptance, essential ingredients for his healing.

The village church was there to support Nick through his wife's illness and his loss of her. This was a very testing time for him, as he struggled with an all-pervading desire for a drink. He wisely returned for counselling sessions at a local support group and it was after one of these sessions that we happened to meet.

Churches should be places of healing, but so often the opposite is true. It is far from easy to get the balance right between faithful teaching of what is right or wrong, what is pleasing to God and what is not, and at the same time showing compassion to those who have fallen short of God's standards. Churches have to be places where we can share our weaknesses and vulnerability and, through a network of support and love, begin to receive healing and restoration.

I believe that within our church communities we should be able to find those with whom we can share our struggles without fear of judgment but in hope of receiving God's healing grace through their love, forgiveness and acceptance. Mercifully God has also provided us with highly trained and skilled professionals dedicated to serve the community. God uses these people, whether or not they are Christians, in miraculous ways to heal our wounds and bring restoration into our lives.

How people can help themselves

Admit the addiction

What helped Nick along the recovery route was the regret he had about the damage his alcoholism had inflicted not only on his own body and mental health but also on his family and on his faith. All this helped him to come out into the open about his problem and do something about it. The relief was enormous.

Go for help

Some are able to break the habit with the support of friends and family but many feel the need to go for professional help. It is important for every addict to find the right help.

Nick went to a local rehabilitation centre to which he had referred some of his own patients. 'Rehab' offers treatment that can greatly reduce or eliminate most of the symptoms of withdrawal from the addictive substance or behaviour. At his first consultation, Nick knew immediately that he had come to the right place for help along the road to recovery. There he found people who stuck by him and also worked with him to explore the root causes of his addiction.

Find a trusted friend

Sometimes the vital first step in acknowledging the problem is admitting it to a trusted friend who can give the necessary support for the next stages of dealing with the situation. Chris's father, whose addiction to pornography had taken such a hold on him, valued enormously the support he received from his pastor. No one else apart from his family knew of his addiction or needed to do so.

How God and the Bible can help

'Wine is a mocker and beer a brawler; whoever is led astray by them is not wise' (Proverbs 20:1). This is one of the many verses in the Bible that condemn drunkenness as well as other vices that separate us from God and are barriers to wholeness of life.

If Paul were alive now he would not mince his words on the addictions that are rampant today and to those caught up in their grip. So often the Christian knows it's wrong and wants to do what is right but can't. As Paul writes, 'I do not understand what I do. For what I want to do I do not do, but what I hate I do. And if I do what I do not want to do, I agree that the law is good. As it is, it is no longer I myself who do it, but it is sin living in me' (Romans 7:15–17). We all have dual personalities: the one that wants to do what is right and the other that jumps out of our sinful nature and wants to control us. For many it is a lifelong battle, but, as Paul says, 'Since we live by the Spirit, let us keep in step with the Spirit' (Galatians 5:25).

Bring the emotional pain to God

So often we know God in a cerebral way, rather than with our hearts, but the Gospel stories are full of emotion, not least in the parable of the lost son (Luke 15:11–32). The reunion between father and son is overwhelming in its emotional force: the father had given his son the freedom which he had asked for, but the son had used it to make unwise and immoral choices. Then one day, hungry and destitute, he decided to return home. He expected rejection and to be treated not as a son but as a servant. Instead we read that 'while he was still a long way off, his father saw him and was filled with compassion for him; he ran to his son, threw his arms around him and kissed him' (v. 20). As we take that first step to turn our backs on the addiction—so crippling in its controlling power—our heavenly Father is there waiting for us with his loving arms outstretched, longing for us to come to him. If we ever fear turning to God, we just need to read this moving story and know that we have nothing to fear, for he is a forgiving father who will embrace us and lead us along the path of healing into wholeness.

Prayer for those struggling with addictive behaviour

Lord Jesus, you came into the world to set us free. I believe that includes freedom from all kinds of addictions. You know how I have tried to break free, but without success. I come to you for deliverance from what makes me so ashamed. I praise you for the freedom you alone can give and trust you for your help from this day on. Amen

Suggestions

- Addicts often return to their addiction when they feel lonely, angry, rejected, tired or sorry for themselves. If you have an addiction from which you need to be released, in addition to professional help, it can make all the difference to have a trusted friend whom you can contact when you feel vulnerable and who can pray for you.
- If you have an addiction from which you long to be released, write a letter to God telling him about your situation and being honest about your feelings. Read it aloud. (You can then destroy it.)
- If you are helping an addict to change their behaviour, help to motivate them by reminding them of the whole picture: the damage to themselves—mind, body and spirit—and to their relationships. Encourage them to hand over their problem to God. It might help to read the story of the lost son (Luke 15:11–32), looking at the father's response to his son when he returned home. Consider being their 'helpline', so that they can contact you in times of temptation.
- If you are aware of someone who won't admit their problem, work out ways in which to help them remove their mask. It might be of value to re-read this chapter and note some of the suggestions made.

- Addictions affect both victim and family, creating difficulties such as communication problems, financial concerns or disturbed children. Work out ways in which the church could give support to a family struggling with addiction-related issues.

Chapter 9

Domestic abuse: lifting the latch

He gives strength to the weary and increases the power of the weak.
ISAIAH 40:29

The ultimate weakness of violence is that it is a descending spiral; returning violence with violence only multiplies violence, adding deeper darkness to a night already devoid of stars. (Martin Luther King)

There is much more media attention given to domestic abuse than ever before and greater recognition of a problem which has been around over the ages. It occurs across the wide spectrum of social classes and is recognised as being just as much prevalent within Christian circles as outside the church. The stigma and shame attached to it, as well as the fear, often prevent victims from removing their masks and seeking help.

William and Mary's story (part 1)

When William and Mary arrived in London from the States they were in their early thirties. They had both lived in Florida all their lives and had met a few years previously at university. William was a financier redeployed from Miami to a job in London. Mary was a nursery teacher who had not been optimistic about obtaining a job in the UK, so she was delighted that soon after her arrival she was accepted as a classroom assistant in a local infant school where Rachel was deputy head. Mary was generally rather quiet and withdrawn, but when there were children around she blossomed.

They started to attend the same church as Rachel. The vicar, keen for congregation members to belong to a home group, identified the one led by Rachel and her husband as a suitable one for them to join. As they met week by week, Rachel began to notice that Mary rarely contributed to any discussion; she was aware that whenever she attempted to say something William would interrupt and talk for her. She also noticed that William was proud to tell others that he had attended a Bible college back in his home town. It was true that he had a good Bible knowledge, but his views were narrow, expressed with a lot of authority and a bit too legalistic for her liking.

Six months after their arrival, Mary phoned into work one day to say she was unwell. Rachel took the call and was concerned for Mary, because she sounded tearful. Mary didn't return to school the next day, so Rachel decided to drop in to see her on the way home. Mary looked pale and Rachel, seeing some bruises on her face, naively enquired whether she had had a fall.

At that moment she heard a key in the lock; William had returned early from work and Mary looked quite fearful. Rachel didn't know what to do. She wanted to help Mary but, sensing some tension between William and Mary, she made her farewells and quietly left, saying she hoped Mary would soon be better and back at school.

What should Rachel do? Both the bruises and the fear she saw on Mary's face when William appeared made her suspect that there had been some physical violence. That William wanted to control and dominate Mary was obvious in the home group. On several occasions she had heard him voice narrow views about submission and headship within a marriage. Rachel even went as far as to look up and reflect on Paul's teaching, 'Wives, submit to your husbands as to the Lord. For the husband is the head of the wife as Christ is the head of the church, his body, of which he is the Saviour' (Ephesians 5:22–23). Rachel knew that William was not too keen on Mary working, for he saw it as a woman's role to stay at home and run the household. Could it be that Mary, who loved her job, was standing up for herself and William, with his somewhat aggressive personality, was using physical force to coerce Mary into submission, justifying his behaviour from Paul's teaching? All this sent shivers down Rachel's spine.

Although she had a hunch that the situation was a serious one, Rachel came to the conclusion that it was probably wiser not to get involved at the moment. Instead, she laid the problem at Jesus' feet, praying specifically for his protection and care of Mary, a working of God's Holy Spirit in William's life and a willingness on Mary's part to share her situation if an opportunity arose to talk together.

This sad story of hidden physical domestic abuse is typical of many that take place across the globe irrespective of age, gender and church allegiance.

What is domestic abuse?

On its website, Women's Aid, a key national charity working towards ending domestic abuse, defines domestic abuse as 'the abuse of a person physically, emotionally, spiritually, socially or psychologically within an intimate or family-type relationship and that forms a pattern of coercive and controlling behaviour'.

We may be able to look back and be conscious of some kind of inappropriate and abusive type of behaviour that has occurred in our family or in families of others—for instance, verbal abuse—but whether it is actual abuse and criminal in the legal sense may be difficult to determine.

A staggering one in twelve people are abused in their lifetime and for many this is on-going. Around 80 per cent of the perpetrators are men. Much abuse goes unreported, especially when it involves a family member. Many people ask why those suffering domestic abuse do not speak up about it and leave the abuser. Obviously shame plays a part in this response, but by far the stronger reason is that, once exposed, the perpetrator's behaviour is likely to become more violent and even murderous, because of their desire for power and control over the other.

Types of domestic abuse

Emotional abuse

Emotional abuse underlies other types of abuse and includes both verbal and non-verbal behaviour. Perhaps the most damaging aspect is the emotional trauma experienced in being cruelly treated by someone with whom there has been, or should have been, mutual love and trust. Victims may not at first recognise what is happening. Early signs may include undue criticism, the victim constantly being put down and humiliated by comments such as 'You can never do anything right!' Shouting, nagging and arguing may also become part of everyday life. Only close members of the family are likely to be aware of what is going on, as the perpetrators choose to abuse where it is safe to do so, for fear of exposure.

Sexual abuse

Sexual abuse within a marriage is one of the least reported forms of abuse and yet it is by no means a rare occurrence. It can occur in marriages where there is intense conflict in the relationship—often accompanied by both verbal and physical abuse—with the man seeking to exercise what he sees as his marital rights, forcing sex on his wife against her will.

William and Mary's story (part 2)

William's abuse of Mary extended to his sexual behaviour. Night after night she was forced to submit her body to his, William claiming this as his marital right and reminding her constantly of her promise on their wedding day to obey him. Their sexual relationship was devoid of any affection, so that Mary felt unable to respond with any warmth to his advances. Although she despised his acts and hated him for them, she told herself that as his wife she had a duty to make herself available to him.

As we have seen, William had a deep-rooted craving to control his wife and their sexual relationship was no exception. Such behaviour is wrong and unacceptable, and no one should have to endure it.

Spiritual abuse

Spiritual abuse can be committed within families and churches by authoritarian and controlling people, like William, who make excessive demands on others to conform to certain types of behaviour against the abused person's beliefs, natural desires and will, justified by theological and biblical arguments. It is not necessarily accompanied by physical abuse.

William and Mary's story (part 3)

William had had a strict Christian upbringing and was narrow in his thinking and in the ways in which he interpreted and applied the Bible. Having been instrumental in Mary becoming a Christian, he felt responsible for her spiritual welfare. One of his favourite verses was from Paul's first letter to Timothy: a woman 'should learn in quietness and full submission' (1 Timothy 2:11); and that is precisely what he required of her. Having been brought up in a non-Christian home and not attending church as a child, Mary had limited knowledge of the Bible, so every day William would force her to learn long passages by heart. Despite Mary's pleadings, television was banned from their home and William restricted the use of their computer. 'Set your minds on things above, not on earthly things,' he would quote (Colossians 3:2) and then tell her that even her desire for worldly belongings was sinful and required repentance. His innate desire was to control her mind, body and soul, forcing her to comply with what he wanted, and all this under the guise of obedience to scripture. He would say that just as Eve was deceived, so women could not to be trusted to do their own thinking but needed guidance from their husbands. At first Mary would try to reason with him, but invariably he would get the better of her in any argument, so she realised that to do what he demanded made life easier and calmer. Gradually she began to believe that the problem was hers and not his; she was his helper and there to meet his needs in the ways he dictated. It was only when she met others, like Rachel and her husband, that she realised how wrong William's attitude and teatment of her actually were.

Financial abuse
Financial abuse is difficult to define; it takes many different forms and there are different levels of intensity. For instance, the husband or wife may say that finances are fine but in fact, for whatever reason, this may be far from the truth. I know of two husbands who forced their wives to submit to the signing of documents to the husbands' financial advantage. Stories abound of wives being kept short of money for housekeeping and then accused of overspending. Some abusers insist that a strict record be kept of all expenditure and then verbally abuse their wives when the results are not to their liking.

Causes of domestic abuse
Faulty theology
As William and Mary's story shows, the Bible can be misunderstood and misused to control another person. Abusers may do this because they have been poorly taught, but there is also likely to be something in their background and/or personality that gives them the desire to exert control over others.

Stress
Situations of stress can easily build up within everyday married life: a child persistently whining or crying, a businessman pressurised at work or a housewife seen by her husband as not coping, are all examples of situations where tensions can build up and—along with other factors—lead to abuse within a family.

Insecurity
One of the factors can be insecurity. A husband may see himself as either less intelligent or less capable (or both) than his wife, and

feel threatened; a power struggle may then develop and in some cases lead to physical abuse by one partner or the other.

Childhood abuse

Children who witness abuse in their parents often become abusers themselves in adulthood. This perspective suggests that domestic violence is learned behaviour with the idea that it is used to resolve matrimonial conflicts. In these cases early intervention with children from violent households may help minimise the risk of further abuse caused by exposure to abusive adult models.

Graham's story

Graham was the only child of two highly intelligent parents who each had high expectations for him. Almost as soon as he was born they put his name down for a well-known public school and in the early formative years of his life he was coerced into achievements and high performance at school. It was demoralising for Graham to be reprimanded when he felt he had done his best but his grades at school still fell short of his father's expectations. 'Your best is not good enough!' he was persistently told. When he rebelled, defending his achievements, he was beaten. Deprived of both love and understanding, his emotional needs remained unmet. Although it was not diagnosed at the time, Graham knows now that the severe depression from which he has suffered most of his adult life set in at an early age. He developed a controlling nature and when he was married became an abuser himself of his wife.

Effects of domestic abuse

The effects of domestic abuse vary according to what caused it, but to be the victim of any type of abuse is a shattering experience and very damaging psychologically. The shame aroused by abuse is often so deep that the victim isn't able to share it with others and so the whole situation festers. Abuse is totally at variance with Jesus' teaching on love and the value of the individual. Paul reminds us that our body is God's temple through his Holy Spirit: 'Do you not know that your body is a temple of the Holy Spirit, who is in you, whom you have received from God?' (1 Corinthians 6:19). John teaches the truth that we can have no love in us for God if we are abusing another: 'And he has given us this command: Whoever loves God must also love his brother' (1 John 4:21).

Feelings

When they are able to express their feelings, victims talk of anger, confusion, helplessness, humiliation and worthlessness. They feel socially isolated from others and, fearful of the consequences, they may keep what is happening hidden for many years—although, it is to be hoped, not for ever.

Psychological disorders

Anxiety and depression are common responses, but victims may be reluctant to go for help, fearing their abuser's possible reaction if they do so.

Distorted thinking

People who are abused can develop distorted thinking about themselves as being worthless, unattractive and unwanted. When this thinking is prolonged it can lead to a sense of low self-worth and loss of identity.

Spiritual repercussions

Questions abused people may ask include: 'Where is God in all this?' 'Why does God allow this to happen?' Not surprisingly they often struggle with doubts, and prayers may well consist of cries for help; they may find it difficult or even impossible to trust God for his protection of them.

How the church can help

Unfortunately, church members can have numerous misconceptions about domestic abuse and how to deal with it. On the one hand, as we have already seen, there are those who cannot understand why the abused person doesn't leave the perpetrator, not fully realising that to do so could increase the anger and lead to escalating violence. On the other hand, some abused people are told that separation and divorce are wrong and that they must stay with the abuser, come what may; this advice may come with reassurance about God bringing good out of suffering and, eventually, giving them a heavenly reward for their obedience.

More helpfully, there is the story of a Christian couple whose relationship was in smithereens after a long episode of physical abuse. The wife was desperate and wisely sought help from their pastor. Fortunately, he did not give them the advice outlined above. Instead he helped them consider separation as well as strategies for trying to save their marriage. They received very intensive counselling, initially individually and subsequently as a couple; this was a harrowing period for each of them. After almost a year, during which time they worked on the major issues that had resulted in the abusive behaviour, they decided to get back together again and this was done with the help of a pastor from another church and their counsellor. Repentance on the part of the abuser and forgiveness by the victim were absolutely vital for them in order to be truly reconciled. It was seen as prudent that the couple should move to a different area and then start attending another church. There has been amazing healing in their lives and they are now living in peace and harmony with each other.

Helplines

As already mentioned, churches have a responsibility to offer up-to-date and accurate information about the help that is available. This can take the form of displays on notice boards of helplines with telephone numbers and websites which people can access easily and without embarrassment (see Resources, p. 176). Churches should check that marriage preparation and marriage enrichment courses include issues of conflict, control and abuse. Preaching and teaching by the leaders can make it clear that any type of controlling behaviour is wrong and should be addressed and stopped.

The churches in my own town have worked together to offer domestic abuse awareness seminars followed by specialist training for those who want to be at the sharp end of victim care. In conjunction with other towns across our county, a safe haven has been established to accommodate victims and their families away from their home locality.

Helping the perpetrator

In any attempt to help the abuser, it must be made clear that their behaviour is wrong and that they alone are responsible for it and not the victim. They must be told that it has to stop and that if they threaten murder, the police will be informed. The abuser has to face up to the harm they are doing and accept that their behaviour must change and forgiveness be sought. Prayer can play a vital part in all of this. Confidentiality about the situation is essential, and if the spouse has left their whereabouts must be protected. Anyone involved in helping has to realise that the abuser is likely to be manipulative; remorse does not necessarily indicate genuine repentance.

How people can help themselves

Going to their GP

Ideally GPs should be the first port of call. The perpetrator may also decide of their own volition to seek help, and ideally the doctor will advise both victims and perpetrators on the best and most appropriate way forward. Understandably, going to their GP is a huge step for all parties concerned.

Sharing the situation with a friend

To find the right person with whom to share the intimate details of a traumatic situation is not always easy. Empathy, understanding and confidentiality are of the essence and sometimes we may prefer to seek out a person not already known to us, on the basis of those qualities. The organisation Christian Listeners is a great resource and can be found in most areas within the UK and beyond (see Resources, p. 176). It offers trained listeners, equipped to be alongside those who want to share their stories, needs and hurts, and may prove a helpful stepping stone towards obtaining professional help.

William and Mary's story (part 4)

Mary was fortunate to find a caring friend in Rachel. Some weeks after that uncomfortable home visit, they met at the doctor's. It was an embarrassing moment as they sat together, staring at a poster about domestic abuse and relevant helplines. Then they found themselves smiling at each other.

Afterwards they met up for coffee and a chat. Mary saw in Rachel a friend in whom she could totally trust. Rachel was a born listener, doing so attentively even when Mary went into some of the more gruesome and humiliating details of her situation.

Leaving the abusive situation

In the end, dealing with an abusive situation usually involves the abused partner leaving the marriage. Whether someone leaves or stays, they will still need support and friendship in many ways over a long period of time.

William and Mary's story (part 5)

Gently Rachel asked whether Mary had ever considered leaving William. Mary told her that was not in her thinking at all; in fact, she didn't feel it was possible. William currently controlled all the money, so she had none of her own. She knew, too, that she had lost so much self-confidence that she wouldn't be able to cope on her own. In her heart of hearts she would love to escape from her present situation and start afresh, but she couldn't see this as a realistic option. She also knew that if she were to leave him his anger would know no bounds.

Rachel realised that first of all Mary had to understand that the way she was being treated was wrong and contrary to Bible teaching. She also had to understand that it was not her fault and she should not be feeling guilty. Rachel emphasised that Mary could choose what she wanted to do. She could choose to take steps for William to be prosecuted for his violent behaviour towards her; she could stay with him or leave. Support, help, advice and even a safe house were all available, but the decision would remain hers.

Despite Mary being adamant that she could not leave William, Rachel gave her details of a safe place where she could go if the situation became dire.

It helped Mary enormously to share what was going on and to be assured of Rachel's love, support and confidentiality. It was liberating to know at last that someone else cared about her and would be praying for her. This sharing was just the beginning of a slow process of healing for her.

How God and the Bible can help

Over the centuries the Bible has been used to justify certain behaviours, not least in the area of submission of wives to husbands. In Mary's case she was physically abused to force her into submission by a controlling husband. William's personality was such that he enjoyed this role and he used an interpretation of Paul's teaching on submission to justify his abusive behaviour: 'Wives, submit to your husbands as to the Lord. For the husband is the head of the wife as Christ is the head of the church, his body, of which he is the Saviour' (Ephesians 5:22–23). John Stott wrote very helpfully in *The Message of Ephesians*: 'The wife's submission is to a lover and not an ogre.' Husbands are not commanded to be cruel to their wives but instead 'husbands ought to love their wives' (Ephesians

5:28). Whatever we are to understand by a loving relationship, submission has to be seen in this context.

No person is more powerless than the victim of abuse. There are wonderful lessons to be learned in the book of Psalms, notably in circumstances of desperation. The setting of Psalm 143 is a cave in which David was hiding from Saul's pursuing enemy—he spent years living as an outlaw in the land God had promised he would one day rule. In this psalm he is overwhelmed by his situation and desperate for help. He pours out his distress to God: 'O Lord, hear my prayer, listen to my cry for mercy: in your faithfulness and righteousness come to my relief' (v. 1). In this psalm (v. 10) and other psalms David frequently speaks of 'my God', indicating a closeness and an intimacy with God. Psalm 144 gives a glimpse of the joy of this intimacy; his imagery describes God as: my rock, my fortress, my stronghold, my deliverer, my shield (vv. 1–2). When we experience God in a personal and intimate way and have a sense of his living presence with us, God expects us to cry out to him, as David did, sharing all the secrets of our hearts and claiming the promise that 'the Lord gives strength to his people; the Lord blesses his people with peace' (Psalm 29:11).

Jesus mirrors compassion and love, and the Gospels are full of stories of forgiveness, healing and wholeness. The Samaritan woman—an adulterer and outcast—met the promised Messiah at the well in Samaria and gave testimony to this. This encounter with Jesus is very powerful; I suggest that it is helpful to read the whole of John 4:1–42 to grasp the full impact of the encounter on the woman's life. The risen Jesus is present with us through his Holy Spirit and longs to bring comfort to those suffering the pain and trauma of abuse.

The message for the abuser is that there is no sin that cannot be forgiven by God; he longs to bring release from the bondage of abusive behaviour and for lives to be rebuilt with him and with others. His Son Jesus knows what it is to suffer pain and die at the hands of cruel abusers. As we come in penitence and faith, resting in the promise that he 'will forgive us our sins and purify us from all unrighteousness' (1 John 1:9), there is just one proviso—that we cannot be fully forgiven unless we are willing to put a stop to the abusive behaviour. As God wipes the slate clean and we start on the road to restoration, it could be helpful and wise to share what is going on confidentially with another person such as a church leader.

Although assured that God has forgiven us, we need to be able to forgive ourselves and work through our own guilt and the associated feelings of confusion and shame. If those who have been wronged and hurt can also forgive us, this can make an enormous impact on those involved. It needs gracious and loving hearts both to offer and to accept forgiveness. Paul tells the Colossians: 'Bear with each other and forgive whatever grievances you may have against one another' (Colossians 3:13). He then goes on in the same chapter (vv. 18–25) to teach rules for Christian households.

God longs for restored relationships. In no way can we reach the level of love required to repair a relationship damaged by abuse without God's help. 'Love is patient, love is kind. It does not envy, it does not boast, it is not proud. It is not rude, it is not self-seeking, it is not easily angered, it keeps no record of wrongs. Love does not delight in evil but rejoices with the truth. It always protects, always trusts, always hopes, always perseveres' (1 Corinthians 13:4–7). A personal relationship with our changeless and forgiving God and a conscious determination to put God at the centre of the home will be vital ingredients for this restoration process.

Prayer for those seeking to support victims of domestic abuse

Loving Father, we pray for a greater awareness of those who suffer domestic abuse and wisdom for those who seek to protect them. Bring your peace to the victims and provide them with loving and supportive friends. For the perpetrators we pray for openness to being helped to overcome their destructive behaviour. Bring healing, forgiveness and restoration into such broken lives through our Lord Jesus Christ. Amen

Suggestions

- In your small group or with a group of friends, work out ways in which you can create within your church an environment in which people feel safe enough to be honest, even about domestic abuse.
- Work out ways in which your church can encourage victims of abuse and the perpetrators to be open about what is happening and seek help.
- What actions could your church and local community take to prevent domestic abuse?
- How has this chapter helped you have a better understanding of domestic abuse?
- Identify verses and passages in the New Testament where non-violence is stressed and retribution prohibited.
- Identify verses and passages in the Bible which, if obeyed, would make domestic abuse totally unthinkable.

Chapter 10

Fear of change: security and identity

Jesus Christ is the same yesterday and today and for ever.
HEBREWS 13:8

Fear of change and its frequent companion anxiety can cripple our lives. The first step out of such disability is honestly facing what we are feeling.

At any stage in life we can be confronted with a major change such as moving house, getting married, or having a first child, a new job or a life-threatening illness. Our reactions to change are influenced by our gender, age, previous experiences and personality. Some can cope, others are fearful. And yet life is always changing—sometimes so slowly that we scarcely perceive it, sometimes in a sudden and profound manner. Fear of change and its frequent companion anxiety can cripple our lives. The first step out of such disability is honestly facing what we are feeling and the next challenge is how to make sense of it and integrate it into our lives. We will learn from one of the stories in this chapter how the experience of change, which initially felt impossible to accept, brought about personal growth. Sometimes, if we allow ourselves to move out of our comfort zone, we might even enjoy a sense of adventure from a change in our situation.

Types of fear of change

A child's reaction to change

In chapter 6 we had a glimpse of what it was like for Sam, a boy of nine, to move house. Even at that young age, in the turmoil of what was going on around him he was reluctant to tell his parents of his fears—he didn't want to upset them. It was only when he began to be bullied at his new school that his fears became a reality: while he still had the love and security that he received from his parents, he had lost much that had been dear and familiar to him, and for this he was ill-prepared. He was confused and felt he had lost the person he had known himself to be.

Parents' reaction to change

Letting go of our children and watching them grow into adulthood and independence can be gratifying for some parents but difficult and painful for others. However easy or difficult this may be, the outcome can be very rewarding, as the parent–child relationship develops into an adult–adult one. This is a time in life when parents begin to re-evaluate marriages no longer held together by the demands of dependent children. In some cases marriages can come under attack; ways may therefore need to be found not just to protect the marriage but to enrich it as the relationship enters a new stage.

Reaction to redundancy

In the present uncertain economic climate, with the threat of wide-spread financial cuts, many have an underlying fear of losing their job. For Richard this became a reality.

Richard's story (part 1)

Richard felt as though he was floating outside his body and noticed his hands were shaking as he pulled open the carrier bag and poured the contents of his desk drawers into it. He snatched up the photograph of his wife and two children from his desk, placed it on the top and tied a knot in the bag.

The lift pinged cheerfully as it deposited Richard on the ground floor. He trudged up to reception—his card key had been confiscated and he needed to ask Janet to let him through the glass exit door. His chest felt tight as he made his way slowly down the busy street towards the station. How could it be that he had left home that morning with everything seemingly normal and by mid-afternoon he no longer had a job on the trading floor? Only six months ago, against much competition, Richard had been promoted within the company; what was more, he had felt pleased with his own performance since then. And now a decision involving sudden cut-backs had been made by the board of directors; he would be placed on 'gardening leave' at home while he worked out his notice period. Twenty-three years of commitment finished in a five-minute conversation with his red-faced boss.

In a haze, Richard retraced his own steps, a journey he'd made on countless occasions. He boarded the train and found a seat facing forwards, the way he always did. How would he find the words to tell his wife, Tessa? Would she be angry? How would they cope as a family? Maybe Tessa would leave him. Richard felt his life was all but over. He was redundant and, in his mind, a failure.

This story is sadly typical in the culture of the business and banking worlds. In industry and the retail sector there can be a collective fear of a company closing down. Richard's fear of redundancy became a reality with all the resultant consequences: networking for a new job, struggling to pay the mortgage, trying to make ends meet, perhaps changing roles with his wife as the breadwinner, anxiety about letting down the family, as well as having to contend with his own low morale and sense of failure. 'It might not happen, so it's better not to share my fears with the family and make them fearful as well,' he had told himself.

Having chatted to a number of workers within the financial world, I have found that among many of them an atmosphere of fear has developed that is having an adverse effect in the workplace. Although most redundancies, especially in larger companies (such as banks), are based on business needs and the jobs are normally filled using a fair selection process, the possibility of being the next victim is nevertheless difficult to face. This can result in an unhealthy competitive spirit among colleagues and affect decision-making, as in the case of a Christian I know who was unsure whether to go for promotion in case there was a 'last in, first out' policy. Long hours of work to combat this situation can have a damaging effect on family life as well as souring workplace relationships. This is a testing time for Christians as they try to trust God for their future and witness to others of God's love and faithfulness.

Fear of lost identity

International companies often require their employees to work abroad. For some this can be an enriching experience; others, particularly the spouses who have no job fulfilment, find difficulty in adjusting to their new environment.

Lisa's story

Lisa made her way out of the church and into the light drizzle, following the small crowd into the adjacent hall. Inside she noticed the musty, alien smell as she joined a line with other members of the congregation eager for coffee. Everyone else seemed to be chatting to someone; Lisa listened intently to their proper English voices and unusual turns of phrase and wondered if she would ever be able to copy them. Placing a couple of pound coins in a pretty china dish, she picked up a small cookie; it felt unusually dry to the touch. Helping herself to a mug of instant coffee, she hesitated, wondering which direction to head in. She nibbled the cookie, glad of a distraction; it was quite nice, but not as rich or as sweet as the ones she was used to back home in America.

A kindly woman spied her standing alone and quickly introduced her to a couple who looked similar to her in age. Exchanging pleasantries about the church service, they chatted a while, but the English women struggled to understand Lisa's southern drawl and soon ran out of things to say. Lisa smiled a half smile to the couple, trying not to prolong their mutual discomfort or show her sadness. 'Oh well, must be gettin' along,' she said as she turned to go. She wondered if she should say goodbye to the vicar and his wife, but having no idea of the protocol she handed in her mug and headed home.

Entering the cool, dark, hallway of her rented house, Lisa noticed her stomach churning with anxiety. Her husband, Larry, was away on business and in the silence of the house she was tearful again. Wiping her damp face, she chastised herself for being morose. She was experiencing an enormous change of lifestyle from her comfort zone in America to England but had hoped that going to church would raise her spirits. Used to attending an Episcopalian church in America, Lisa had heard that the order of service and liturgy in the Church of England were very similar. So why did it feel so difficult to make a connection with God here or to fit in with folks? Lisa swallowed hard, trying to push down the lump in her throat. She sensed she was angry, but did not understand why.

She sighed to herself. Everything felt different here—not just the cool climate and the tiny roads or the look and feel of the church; even the hymns were set to different music. People did not seem to 'get her' here and she felt weird and isolated. Normally a confident, happy person, Lisa no longer recognised herself three months into the posting from Louisiana to Kent. Would she ever adjust to the differences between the two cultures? She was scared she might lose part of herself in the process. 'Who am I anyway?' she asked herself. It was then that she realised she could not locate her sense of who she was any more. With no friends, family or neighbours to chat to and no role of any kind, she felt she wasn't living—she was just about existing.

Nowadays global travel and job opportunities are commonplace and it is not unusual for people in Lisa's situation to find themselves suffering from culture shock and identity crisis. With the cornerstones of Lisa's life changed overnight, she was left angry, confused, homesick and longing for all that was familiar. She needed more time to adjust to the different culture in England but also the care and understanding of others to help her normalise what she was experiencing and make a successful transition.

Fear of death and dying

Most churches are at pains to care for the elderly—this may involve visiting the housebound or taking services in care homes—but how many build meaningful bridges of friendship so that the emotional and spiritual concerns are shared?

Anita's story (part 1)

Anita had worked with her husband as a missionary in Ghana for over 30 years and her life had been fulfilling and enjoyable. When her husband developed cancer at the age of 60 and required surgery, they returned to England. For the next two years, as his condition gradually deteriorated, she devoted herself to his care until he was taken into the hospice where he died. During that time they talked openly together about death and dying and even prepared his funeral service down to the smallest detail.

In the early days of bereavement, Anita was well supported in practical ways by her church and appeared to be coping well. However, her brother Jack was aware that she was becoming withdrawn and quite depressed. When questioned, Anita confessed to feeling spiritually low and confused. In truth she had come face to face with the reality and the inevitability of Jack's death and was fearful of it. 'No-one needs or depends on me any more,' she told her brother. Anita even wondered whether anything she had done in her lifetime mattered to anyone now. She also had a strong fear of the pain and suffering that she had seen Jack experience in his dying weeks. And her on-going doubts had turned into a fear that God didn't exist and that the faith she had practised over the years had been founded on a myth. Anita was still going through the motions of being a Christian—regularly attending church as well as her mid-week home group—but these fears which she dared not share were beginning to overwhelm her. She was nostalgic for her past; ahead was a fearful unknown from which she could see no means of escape.

Anita had been so immersed first in her work as a missionary and then in her care of her husband that she was left ill-prepared to start facing the prospect of her own dying. This story and others suggest that there are many older people in our church communities who are fearful of death but have no one close enough with whom they feel they can share their feelings.

Effects of fear of change

Lost expectations

In each of these stories, we see how a sudden change of circumstances generates fear because the individuals concerned are pushed into situations beyond their personal control. When Richard was made redundant, he was full of pessimism and anxiety, unable to see anything positive in the immediate future. As he returned to his home on the evening of his redundancy, head hanging low, he felt very much like a lost soul.

Richard's story (part 2)

It was about three weeks later that Richard became completely stuck. By then the full magnitude of his situation had settled over him like a pool of black treacle. He found himself unable to do anything, feel anything; all purpose seemed lost. He could not even be bothered to get washed in the morning. 'What is the point?' a voice in his head kept saying. His motivation to get up and face the day had gone, along with his sense of identity as a successful city worker.

When he finally went for therapy, Richard admitted to feeling angry with himself—why had he not seen that redundancy was really coming? He was also angry with the company for which he'd worked so hard. He told the therapist that he now felt that all his extra work at weekends had been a waste of precious time. He was clearly dispensable and felt sure he would never work again.

Richard needed the support of his therapist to help him make sense of these spiralling thought patterns, to acknowledge his shock and to understand his pain.

Eventually he was able to offer himself some compassion and move ahead with his life. One year on, Richard was fit and well. He had adjusted to a different lifestyle, working for himself and setting up his own business, using his considerable knowledge of computer systems to provide services for which people were willing to pay. His income was, at least for the moment, much reduced but his redundancy pay had taken care of his mortgage and now that his confidence had returned he was sleeping much better than before and leading a less stressful life. His wife and children enjoyed having him around more and he felt a stronger connection with them. He was also able to attend church regularly and enjoy the support and fellowship of a home group.

Richard would not have chosen to end his city career in such an abrupt manner but he could see now that the imposed change had brought some good outcomes and personal learning and growth.

It was a long haul for Richard and his family and he struggled more than some to come to terms with his changed circumstances. As he worked through his anger and resentment with the help of his therapist, he began to be galvanised into action and was able to build himself a new life, one that was more productive and fulfilling.

Lost identity

It was only when Lisa was actually in a different country, in unfamiliar territory, that she became distressed, having no one to turn to who understood her loneliness and fears. Up till then she had had a zest for life; now her identity seemed to have disappeared, along with her sense of belonging, and she struggled to know who she was. Lisa needed to rebuild her sense of identity slowly and adjust to her changed circumstances. This was as scary for her as it had been for Sam, the nine-year-old who had moved house and faced being bullied at his new school.

Lost hope

Anita was suffering deep grief and the pain of bereavement following the death of her husband. She spiralled into depression and seemed no longer able to draw strength from her faith. Feeling alienated from God, her own fear of death became very real too.

How the church can help

Ideally the church should provide support for those suffering a crisis of identity after a profound change in their lives. As mentioned earlier, a kindly, welcoming attitude is part of the church's role in helping those who are emotionally stressed. It is important to remember that even though people appear to be coping, they are often hurting inside. Asking them how they are is a good open question if followed by a sincere listening response. For example, asking Lisa how she found living in another country could have given her the chance to open up a little and acknowledge that she was not finding it easy.

Linking new people with others in a similar situation or finding a suitable home group or Bible study group for them can help towards integrating them in the church family.

The church also needs to look out for people like Richard, in his situation of redundancy, offering a listening ear and considering appropriate ways in which to offer help.

Anita was obviously suffering exhaustion through caring for her husband and then trying to come to terms with life without him. The whole experience had aged her and now she was struggling to face her future alone. Emotionally drained and physically weary, she had plummeted into a depressed state. This was a time when, more than ever before, she needed other Christians to support and care for her. Her home group may well have helped her in practical ways, but more important than this was her need for a meaningful conversation and someone with whom she could share her deepest thoughts and anxieties. The church has a clear responsibility in ministering to the spiritual and emotional needs of older people who have lost their previous identity in life, for whatever reason, and are struggling to accept the new one. To draw alongside these people and listen to their experiences of life and their current concerns about change and lost identity can help them to see who they really are: precious members of Christ's body, to be valued, cherished and encouraged to continue to lead meaningful lives.

A church family comes especially into its own for those who have no immediate family, as seen in Cyril's situation.

Cyril's story—a 'good ending'

In his late 90s, Cyril had what might be described as a 'good ending'. Having no immediate family, the church played a significant role during the last years of his life following the death of his wife. In many ways he had had a sad life, and the church family brought fresh meaning, hope and enjoyment into it, showing him in many different ways the love of Jesus. With one person he shared two of his fears: one was dying alone and the other was a spiritual burden that he had carried over many decades. Although he understood the meaning of the cross, he still felt unworthy of his place in heaven. Three relatively young people from the church were alongside in his final days in hospital. The day before his death he was very restless and fearful. However, the next day when one of the chaplains was called to his bedside, things took what was later described as a miraculous turn. Taking Cyril's hand, the chaplain quietly prayed that he would lay at the foot of the cross any burden he was carrying and claim Jesus' forgiveness. Those gathered around the bedside saw a look of peace and joy spread across Cyril's face as he at last let go of his burdens. He was not dying alone, for his loving church family were alongside him; he knew at last he had received forgiveness and he was ready to meet his Saviour in heaven. This he did not long afterwards.

Once alerted to Anita's fears and struggles, her church was able to give her the helping hand she needed.

Anita's story (part 2)

Anita's brother alerted her church minister to the depression she was suffering. He put her in touch with a missionary who was home from Thailand visiting her family. Over the following weeks they chatted over numerous cups of tea and biscuits. It was like a breath of fresh air for Anita to be able to share her fears and feelings openly and to be listened to and understood. Through the love and compassion that she received, she gradually began to acknowledge that God was still there for her, realising that his existence didn't depend on her feelings.

How people can help themselves

Sharing

When our circumstances change dramatically, adjustment can be a significant struggle. Sharing concerns with a trusted friend or family member can help us to accept the changes, however big they are, and integrate them into a new identity—our sense of who we are. It might help to seek out those who are in a similar situation, possibly a support group of some kind. Sometimes people will need a professional therapist to help them make sense of it all. Talking therapy allows somebody to offload without fear of embarrassment or repercussions and provides a safe place to express uncomfortable feelings.

Writing

As well as finding somebody to talk to, people can benefit from writing their feelings down in a journal. Throughout the day we have thousands of thoughts occupying our minds, most of which come and go in a second. These thoughts will link us to memories, often the same ones being replayed over and over again. The result can be that we reinterpret how we feel based on repetitive ways of thought processing. By writing down these thoughts on paper, we can observe what is happening and develop alternative ways of thinking.

How God and the Bible can help

The changed circumstances of each of the individuals in the above stories were quite radical, transferring them out of their comfort zones and into the exile of unfamiliar territories. Such situations were not unknown in biblical times. Daniel, the prophet and interpreter of dreams, was taken into exile with friends from Jerusalem and ended up in the court of Babylon, being trained for the king's service. To have been selected for this elite training must have been seen as a great privilege and opportunity, but the exile was still permanent, with his home and family, traditions, culture and rituals of worship of his God stripped away.

Sometimes the circumstances are a deliberate choice (such as withdrawal from an unsuitable relationship or a change of life in pursuit of a particular calling), yet even those require adjustment. Moses gave up his identity as the son of Pharaoh's daughter, with all the wealth and status it offered, to be identified with the people of God. He placed his life in God's hands and was used powerfully to lead the Israelites out of captivity in Egypt into the promised land. It is our identity as God's children that must govern our lives and draw us towards the true blessings that God has in store for us.

The writer to the Hebrews reminds us of the promise of God, 'Never will I leave you; never will I forsake you', to which we respond, 'The Lord is my helper; I will not be afraid' (Hebrews 13:5–6). We need to remember that in God we possess everything. We can lose our job, move home, suffer bereavement, but when God is with us we can enjoy ultimate security. However much our circumstances may change, we have the same God, the same Bible and the same Jesus on whom we can totally rely. 'Jesus Christ is the same yesterday and today and for ever' (Hebrews 13:8).

So as we encounter countless changes along life's journey, some dictated for us but others a deliberate choice on our part, it is important to try to keep afloat even when things feel turbulent. This requires understanding and the knowledge of where we are before God and working towards having a strong sense and knowledge of our identity as his child and a member of his kingdom. At the same time, we can resolve to live lives pleasing to God, shaped by his values and standards. We have a changeless God, so our security is found by being anchored within a total commitment to him.

Prayer for those fearful of change

O God, thank you that we can cast all our cares on you because you care for us. I name my fears and anxieties to you… Open my eyes to your resources for me through prayer and reading your word and through the people who can help me. Help me to grow in confidence and peace as I learn to be rooted in you. Thank you that you accept and love me just as I am: flawed and floundering. May I rest in the promises that you are the same, yesterday, today and for ever and that you are with me in every circumstance. Amen

Suggestions

- Reflect on a past experience of change in your life which was initially hard for you and made you fearful. Consider what you have learned through it.
- Consider ways in which your church could help and support those who have (a) experienced a sudden change to their lives such as being made redundant, (b) suffered a significant loss such as the death of a loved one or (c) experienced one of the family leaving home.
- Does your church have a policy of welcoming into your fellowship new people who have moved into the area? If so, how is it working and are there ways in which it could be improved?
- How well are older people, who may be struggling to come to terms with ageing, integrated into the life of your church? Are there ways in which this could be improved?
- 'Is change something to be feared or embraced?' Get together a small group of friends to discuss this. Using your own experiences or those of others known to you might be a helpful basis for your discussion.

Source references

1   John Stott, *The Message of Ephesians* (IVP, 1984), p. 148.

2   Steve Brown, *When Your Rope Breaks*, (Baker Books, 1982).

3   Matthew Johnstone, *Living with a Black Dog: His name is depression* (Andrews McMeel, 2006).

4   Max Lucado, *Every Day Deserves a Chance: Wake up to the gift of 24 hours* (Thomas Nelson, 2007).

5   John White, *Parents in Pain* (IVP, 1979)

6   Daphne du Maurier, quoted in Agnes Whitaker (ed.), *All in the End is Harvest: An anthology for those who grieve* (DLT, 1984)

Bibliography

Addictions

Andre Radmall, *Insight into Addiction* (CWR, 2009)
Tim Chester, *Captured by a Better Vision: Living porn-free* (IVP, 2010)
Peter Gladwin, *Out of the Ashes: The restoration of a burned boy* (recovery from gambling, drink and drugs) (Lion Hudson, 2012)

Depression

Andrew and Elizabeth Procter, *Encountering Depression: Frequently asked questions answered for Christians* (SPCK, 2012)
Matthew Johnstone, *Living with a Black Dog: His name is depression* (Andrews McMeel Publishing, 2006)
Michael Lawson, *D is for Depression: Spiritual, psychological and medical resources for healing depression* (Christian Focus, 2006)
John White, *The Mask of Melancholy: A Christian psychiatrist looks at depression and suicide* (IVP, 1982)

Domestic abuse

Lundy Bancroft, *Why Does He Do That? Inside the minds of angry and controlling men* (Berkeley, 2002)

Financial matters

Rob Parsons, *The Money Secret* (Hodder & Stoughton, 2005)

Identity

Dick Keyes, *Beyond Identity* (Hodder & Stoughton, 1984)
Vernon White, *Identity* (SCM Press, 2002)
Graham Beynon, *Mirror Mirror: Discover your true identity in Christ* (IVP, 2008)

Listening

Michael Mitton, *A Heart to Listen: Becoming a listening person in a noisy world* (BRF, 2004)
Michael Jacobs, *Swift to Hear* (SPCK, 1985)
Anne Long, *Listening* (Darton, Longman and Todd, 1990)

Loneliness

Elisabeth Elliot, *The Path of Loneliness* (Kingsway, 2007)

Loss

Albert Y. Hsu, *Grieving a Suicide* (IVP, 2002)

Gerald Sittser, *A Grace Disguised* (Zondervan, 2004)

Eddie Askew, *Walking into the Light: A journey through grief in poems, prayers and thoughts* (TLM, 2010)

Jean Watson, *Bereavement: Bible readings for special times* (BRF, 2005)

Agnes Whitaker (ed.), *All in the End is Harvest: An anthology for those who grieve* (DLT, 1984)

Marriage

Nicky and Sila Lee, *The Marriage Book* (Alpha International, 2009)

Rob Parsons, *Loving Against the Odds: For every man and every woman in every marriage* (Hodder & Stoughton, 2010)

Harry Benson, *Mentoring Marriages* (Monarch, 2005)

Timothy Keller, *The Meaning of Marriage: Facing the complexities of commitment with the wisdom of God* (Hodder & Stoughton, 2011)

Parenting

Nicky and Sila Lee, *The Parenting Book* (Alpha International, 2009)

John White, *Parents in Pain* (IVP, 1979)

Rob Parsons, *Getting Your Kids Through Church Without Them Ending Up Hating God* (Monarch/Lion Hudson, 2011)

Self-esteem

Chris Ledger and Wendy Bray, *Insight into Self-Esteem* (CWR, 2006)

Joanna & Alister McGrath, *Self-Esteem: The cross and Christian confidence* (IVP, 2001)

Julia Cole, *Loving Yourself, Loving Another: The importance of self-esteem for successful relationships* (Relate Guides, 2008)

General interest

Adam S. McHugh, *Introverts in the Church* (IVP, 2009)

Tim Chester, *You Can Change* (IVP, 2008)

Gary Chapman, *The Five Love Languages* (Northfield, 2004)

Resources

- Cruse Bereavement Care: PO Box 800, Surrey TW9 1RG; www.cruse.org.uk
- Marriage preparation and marriage enrichment courses: Holy Trinity Brompton, Brompton Road, London SW7 1JA; www.htb.org.uk
- Relationship issues: Relate; www.relate.org
- Care for the Family: Garth House, Leon Avenue, Cardiff CF15 7RG; www.careforthefamily.org.uk
- Association of Christian Counsellors: 20 Momus Boulevard, Coventry CV2 5NA; www.acc-uk.org
- Christian Listeners: Acorn Christian Healing Foundation, Whitehill Chase, High Street, Bordon, GU35 0AP; www.acornchristian.org

Addictions

- Alcoholics Anonymous: National Helpline 0845 769 7555; www.alcoholics-anonymous.org.uk
- Alcohol detox: Linwood Park, Wensley Road, New Lodge, Barnsley SY1 1TJ; 0800 915 1560
- For family and friends of alcoholics: www.al-anonuk.org.uk
- For help with internet temptation: www.covenanteyes.com
- Gamblers Anonymous: www.gamblersanonymous.org.uk
- For sexual addiction: http://saa-recovery.org.uk

Domestic abuse

- For women: www.womensaid.org.uk; 0808 2000 247
- For men: www.mensadviceline.org.uk; 0808 801 0327

Others

- Citizens Advice: www.citizensadvice.org.uk
- Samaritans: www.samaritans.org; 08457 909090
- Penhurst Retreat Centre, The Manor House, Penhurst, nr Battle, TN33 9QP; www.penhurst.org.uk